T0171285

VOICES OF MY SOUL

VERSES
AND
MEDITATIONS

BY
Prince John Chaber

Order this book online at www.trafford.com
or email orders@trafford.com

Most Trafford titles are also available at major online book retailers.

Printed in Victoria, BC, Canada.

ISBN: 978-1-4269-2902-1 (soft)
ISBN: 978-1-4269-2903-8 (hard)

Library of Congress Control Number: 2010902921

*Our mission is to efficiently provide the world's finest, most comprehensive book publishing
service, enabling every author to experience success. To find out how to publish your book, your
way, and have it available worldwide, visit us online at www.trafford.com*

Trafford rev. 3/23/2010

 www.trafford.com

North America & international
toll-free: 1 888 232 4444 (USA & Canada)
phone: 250 383 6864 ♦ fax: 812 355 4082

Contents

PART II

THOUGHTS AND MEDITATIONS

PART III
PEOPLE I MET

PART IV
A TRIBUTE TO MOTHERS

PART V
VOICES OF THE HEART

PART VI

Forward

By
The Author

If I could but embark on a time machine capable of taking me back into the past, I would journey all the way in time to a certain valley, the village of my youth.

There, I would bare my soul before my Maker and at the very first faint flutter of my heart, betokening that the time was at hand when it must needs quiver to the haunting melody of love, as is the way of all flesh, I would then, with the care and dedication of a midwife getting ready to receive a new born babe search every nook and cranny, every mountain, hill, dale and valley, until I located a special little flower.

A flower, as fresh as the early morning dew in springtime; a flower whose sweet fragrance, yet un-savored, except by the unbridled innocence of a gentle breeze, lies snugly enveloped by the intimate embrace of her tiny petals.

I would then, with gallant, but tender hands, gently pluck that flower from its bed of sweet repose and after caressing and fondling it briefly, but most intimately, lock it firmly within the innermost chambers of my pounding heart, there to reign forever, my Queen, my friend, my sweetheart, my companion for life, to live in a palace all her own, be it ever so humble.

But, alas, there are no time machines. And time itself does not have a stop. Time marches inexorably on, and so must humans.

"For as a flame once dead cannot burn,
So our youth once fled does not return.
The path we follow, leads but to the grave.
Each breath we take leaves one less to live."

And so my young friends, I caution you, cast not your pearls before swine. I most especially implore and exhort you not to take flowers plucked by the hand of another. For in them may be concealed, hidden thorns, that may pierce even to the depth of your very soul, causing you unspeakable pain and ceaseless suffering and torment.

Do not take flowers from other men's gardens, or from the wayside, or from the common field. And most important of all, never, never, steal them; and never buy them either. Other men's flowers should remain with other men.

For as a flower plucked cannot its life retain,
So its sap once sucked, ought but death remain.

If a flower has been discarded, than let it wither and die. For better it dies alone, unloved, un-wooed, unwanted, than to die, as die it eventually must, killing or wounding you in the process.

Believe me my friends, the best you can expect from men's flowers, plucked by other men's hands, is but an ephemeral and illusory gratification.

But any such gratification will be, of a truth, offset by fretful days and sleepless nights a plenty; and then, finally, a heart so scarred and a life so full of misery, that you will begin to doubt the efficacy of life itself.

Your very existence would seem measured only by the amount of pain you are able to endure. And, there is no pain like the pain of knowing that, it was purchased at a price.

What price would a man not gladly pay,
To have a shot at life again!
And though he dreams his life away,
All his dreams are but in vain!

Flowers from the wayside, or common field, all have the distinct disadvantage of being battered and bruised by every wayfarer and passing traffic; and beside, are usually those already passed over or discarded by those who have chanced along that way before you. The resulting scars are often too indelible to be erased even by the most tender and loving care.

So the affections of tender passion belong to the time when those passions, like nuggets of gold were first separated from the warm, fleshy bowels of mother earth, and plucked by the eager, trembling, hands of the lucky assayer, so, the sweet fragrance and passionate tenderness of a flower belong to those first unforgettable moments, when in the full, fiery passion of its bloom, it fell captive to unsteady fingers eager to embrace its tender innocence and take the first cautious sip of its sweet untainted nectar.

Stolen flowers, or those bought at a price, are in fact other men's flowers that now belong to you, albeit in name only. For you will never know the sweetness of its blushing fragrance when it was a blooming flower, nor pluck from its wooers heart its captured freshness imprisoned there forever.

Never-the-less, my earlier injunction, is again here repeated. Never take other men's flowers, neither for love nor for money. They are seldom what they seem. Often they have already began to fade but are made to appear without spot or blemish by an all too apparent artificiality, which subterfuge you could have easily unmasked, if only you would have taken the time to examine them closely.

A deceitful woman may tell you that, "stolen waters are sweet, and bread eaten in secret is pleasant;" but what she does not reveal is that, "her house is the habitation of the dead, and her guests live in torment in the bowels of hell."

My friends, even if stolen waters are sweet, I assure you that such sweetness is often more imagined than real. In time you will discover that stolen flowers are nothing more than festering lilies. And, in the words of the immortal Poet,

> "Sweetest things, turn sourest by their deeds.
> Lilies that fester, smell far worse than weeds."

This point was best made by one of our ancient philosophers, with his usual sagacious eloquence when he said:-

> "If we could live without women, gentlemen,
> we would save ourselves the bother. But
> nature has ordained that while life with them
> is not easy, life without them would be
> impossible. We must, therefore, live with a view
> towards our future well being and not just for
> the pleasure of the moment."

But my friends, even if it may be that there is sweetness yet remaining in the flower of another, let me assure you that the flower obtained by your own labour of love, is far sweeter and the rewards far more enduring, than any that you may obtain in any other way. "For, it is the hope of reward that sweetens labour."

What sayeth the Ancient of Days about the flowers with which we choose to decorate our lives? Speaking to us through the voice of Wisdom, He says:-

"Drink waters out of thine own cistern, and
running waters out of thine own well. Let
them be only thine own, and not for strangers
with thee. Let thy fountains be blessed and
rejoice with the wife of thy youth."

In another place he admonishes, as I implore you now, "Live joyfully with the wife whom thou loveth all the days of the life of thy vanity; for that is thy portion in this life; and in thy labor, which thou takest under the sun."

Believe me, dear friends, there are plenty of pretty, chaste, un-plucked, flowers out there in nature's own garden, all waiting to be caressed by the trembling fingers of love-tuned souls and eager hearts, pulsating to the vibrating chords of the haunting melody of love. And as things are these days, it is just as well.

The poet was not exaggerating when he wrote:-

"Full many a gem of purest ray serene,
The dark unfathomed caves of oceans bear.
Full many a flower, is born to blush unseen,
And waste its sweetness on the dessert air."

Hark all ye incontinent young lovers, and take careful note. To be fore-warned is to be fore-armed. A word to the wise, they say, is usually enough.

Chose carefully every flower,
That would decorate your life,
The choice you make will ever,
Bring you joy or grief.
And choose you must, so choose aright,
Choose while it is yet day.
Never gather flowers in the night,
It matters not what others say.
Roses, daises, forget-me-nots,
Whatever be your choice,
As long as they're not other men's
That's my main advice.
I met a man the other day,
He was eighty three,
He plucked a flower barely twenty,
But was happy as could be.
I met this other gentleman,
Bought flowers at the country fair.
Each time he breathed, another thorn,
Pierced his heart and brought despair.
I'll borrow here, just one more quote,
And then my friends, I'm done.
T'was Goldsmith's cat, he aptly wrote,
How in a tub it drowned.
The moral of that story was?
Tis as plain as could be.
So let the catch be your own flowers,
And now I quote, wrote he.
"Not all that tempts your wandering eyes,
Or heedless hearts, is lawful prize.
Nor all that glitters, gold!"

Arrangement

Part I, of this book contains sonnets written for the most part from experiences of my own heart. In deciding to publish them, my primary purpose is a desire to share with the reader, the beauty of this type of Elizabethan poetry which I like very much and which I also enjoyed performing.

If there is perceived in them an underlying core of dreary bitterness, melancholy, sadness, or pain, weep not for me. Rather rejoice with me even though you may not be able to share the subliminal ecstasy I have experienced and enshrined within the pleasure and the pain. For where love is there is always joy, ecstasy and bliss. But there are also the corresponding companions of heartache, sorrow and pain. Always bearing in mind, however, that love and hate often live together in the same house.

Remember, too, that there's no pleasure without pain. It is the sweet juice of the grape, mixed with the sour elements of fermentation that combine to make the most perfectly blended wine.

If love was a bed of Roses, then roses would have no more efficacy than the common weed that abound by the wayside and is trodden under the feet of men.

On the other hand,

Where love abounds, there must always be,
Some little wisp of joy, whatever its paucity.

Of a truth, love has lifted me to the highest pinnacle of blissful ecstasy, elevated me and fed me with the sweetest nectar of life; but, at the same time, it has dashed me to the ground, tossed me in the deepest pit, spat upon me and left me there to die a slow, painful, lonely and ignominious death.

The bottom line is, however, I love these sonnets. Whatever may be perceived to be the motivation behind their penning, it would be fair to plead, a certain amount of poetic license. The cup from which the poet drinks is often filled with wine not made with hands. And the parchment on which he chooses to capture the flashing images that inhabit the house of his dreams, cannot be seen with the naked eye or daubed with ought but the brush of his own imagination.

Most of these have been written over forty years ago, and so, may well reflect the seeds of youthful indiscretion. But others are the fruits of riper years. It is my sincerest wish that you will love them too, and that one or more of them will duly become your heart's dearest friend and your life's constant companion.

The other verses are, also, rather special. Wisdom has been with me for a long time. It was written way back in 1963. The Nihilism was written in the late sixties, was lost recaptured, rehashed and extended in more recent times.

Emerald Serenade has been set to music and is really a patriotic song about the country of my birth, which I love with a passion. It has been performed on several occasions by a choral group at their annual music festivals.

Yesterday, Today and Tomorrow, is of course allegorical and introspective. But the truth is we are today what we were yesterday and will be tomorrow. There is much wisdom in the Spanish proverb which says. "Man is as God made him; but sometimes worse."

The Preacher says, "All is vanity...for that which has been, it is that which shall be; and that which is done, is that which shall be done; and there is no new thing under the sun. Is there anything whereof it may be said, See this is new? It hath been already of old time which is before us."

People I met is of course retrospective and so, is a fairly recent creation, although some of the stimuli were long embedded in the deeper regions of the id. But I must warn that nothing written herein is intended to refer to, or reflect on, any person living or dead, and any supposed similarity, including any descriptions or epithets which may appear to allude to any such persons are purely coincidental.

I have taken the liberty of including some materials which are somewhat personal, if not sensitive, including some tributes to my children, my wife and my mother. But I do hope that the reader will advert his critical mind to their poetic content or inherent merit or lack of it, and excuse any apparent indiscretion.

In addition with my wife Elsa's permission, I have chosen to include here a piece, "Saint Who?" which has been previously published elsewhere under her name.

Tribute to mothers is what it says, a tribute to the brave ladies of the world whose role in history and whose contribution to society and every nation to which they belong can never be over emphasized or adequately repaid; for without mothers, there would be no sons. And without sons, civilization would just cease to be.

The Road to Calvary has been explained in tandem. Suffice it to say that every word written herein is an expression of the voice of my soul, especially at those times and during those periods when in agony or ecstasy, joy or sorrow, it cries out to me that my joy is my sorrow, that my light is my darkness, that my today is really tomorrow, that my tomorrows are my yesterdays, that my awakening is my sleeping, that my love is my hate, that my friend is my enemy, that my fullness is my emptiness, that my toil is my rest, that my giving is my receiving, that my marrying is my separation, that my pleasure is my pain, that my loss is my gain, that my life is my death, that my burial is my resurrection.

I do hope that the reader will derive as much pleasure reading this book as I have had in writing it.

Prince John Chaber

WISDOM

WISDOM IS THE FRUIT OF LIFE,
AND A FOOL HE THAT DOUBTS IT.
WEALTH'S THE OFFSPRING, WISDOM THE WIFE,
WE CANNOT LIVE WITHOUT IT.

THE BARDS, THE POETS, THOSE MEN OF OLD,
WHO WROTE WITH INSPIRATION;
LEFT GIFTS OF WISDOM, NOT THE GOLD,
THAT DAMNS OUR GENERATION.

LET PROSPERITY LIVE! BUT IN ITS WAKE
LET WISDOM WEAR THE CROWN.
THE MONARCH THAT WILL NEVER BREAK,
HIS THRONE OF LEARNING DOWN.

WHERE WEALTH ACCUMULATES, MEN DOTH DECAY,
WROTE ONE MORE VERSED THAN I.
BUT WHERE WISDOM WIELDS ITS REGAL SWAY,
ITS LIMITS ARE THE SKY.

Prince John Chaber

FIRST LOVE

YOU VOWED YOU WOULD LOVE ME ALWAYS
MY LOVE. HOW CAN I E'ER FORGET IT?
AND SO MY LOVE, I'LL ALWAYS WAIT,
FOR YOU MY ROSE, BE IT A HUNDRED YEARS.
DO YOU REMEMBER WHEN FIRST WE MET,
HOW EXCITING LOVE HAD BEEN?
AH, TO THIN THAT YOU COULD E'ER FORGET,
MY DARLING, SWEETEART, QUEEN!
AND WAS IT NOT A BLUSHING ROSE,
A BRIGHT RED SWEETLY SCENTED FLOWER,
I PLUCKED FROM ITS BED OF GAY REPOSE,
AND BROUGHT YOU AS MY DOWER?
OH, MAY ITS FRAGRANCE LINGER ON,
ALL THROUGH THE YEARS MY LOVE MY OWN.

Prince John Chaber

SWEET THOUGHTS

EACH TIME I THINK OF LOVE, I THINK OF YOU;
AND WISH THAT FORTUNE'S SCHEMING HAND
WOULD JOIN US BY SOME SOLEMN BOND,
TOGETHER IN A LOVE SINCERE AND TRUE.
COULD YOU BE THINKING THUS OF ME SWEETHEART?
COULD SUCH WARM OVELINESS BE MINE?
COULD ALL THE PLEASURES THAT YOUR LOVE IMPART,
KEEP GLAD MY HEART AND NEVER NEVER END!
EACH MOMENT WHILE WE ARE APART,
TIME SEEMS ENDLESS AS A DAY,
LONG SPENT, AND, COUNTING FROM THE START,
IS NOW A HUNDRED DREARY YEARS AWAY.
MY THOUGHTS OF YOU ARE EVER LOOKING ON,
TO THAT SWEET DAY WHEN ALL MY CARES ARE GONE.

Prince John Chaber

ABSENT LOVE

TONIGHT MY LOVE, I CANNOT BEAR TO THINK,
HOW EMPTY NOW MY LIFE HAS BEEN.
AND LITTLE FAIRIES, ALL MARRILY UNSEEN,
LAUGH AND JEER AND MOCK.
TONIGHT NO WARMTH OF LOVE I FEEL.
NO MOONLIGHT WALKS AND LAUGHTER.
TONIGHT NO KISSES MY LIPS TO SEAL,
NOR COUNTRY FROLICS AFTER.
FOR NOW MY LOVE IS FAR AWAY,
AND LAND AND SEA DIVIDE US.
BUT I'M HOPING THAT SOME SWEET DAY,
WE'LL FIND A WARM TOGETHERNESS.
SOME DAY WE SHALL, WITH HAPPY HEARTS AND TRUE,
FIND A NEW STORE OF LOVE, A BLISSFUL HAVEN TOO!

Prince John Chaber

LOVE'S VISION

OH MY LOVE; THOUGH YOU ARE TONIGHT,
A MILLION MILES AWAY FROM ME,
I LOOK THROUGH SPACE AND I CAN SEE,
OUR LOVE STAR GAILY SHINING BRIGHT.
THROUGH CLOUDS OF DARKNESS IT APPEARS,
IN ALL ITS GLORY FAR ABOVE;
AND MAY ITS BRIGHTNESS THROUGH THE YEARS,
LIGHT THE PATH THAT LEADS TO LOVE.
YESTERDAY MY HART WAS FULL OF CARES.
MY SWEETHEART DID NOT WRITE TO ME.
BUT HOW YOUR LETTER DROVE AWAY MY TEARS,
AND NOW THERE'S JOY AND PEACE AND ECSTASY.
OH STAR OF LOVE, COMPANION OF MY HEART,
SHINE UPON ME AND MY SWEETHEART.

Prince John Chaber

TROUBLED THOUGHTS

MY TROUBLED THOUGHTS, IN DEEP CONFUSION, SEEK
ALONG LIFE'S TIRESOME BEATEN PATH,
TO FIND A LOVER FOR A BROKEN HEART.
A HEART LONG TREMBLING ON THE BRINK,
OF UTTER, HOPELESS, DESOLATION.
OF CEASELESS TEARS, BY NIGHT AND DAY.
A HEART FORLORN, AND WHOSE ONLY CONSOLATION,
IS THAT TOMORROW MAY END THE CARES OF TODAY.
BUT EACH DAY BRINGS ITS OWN TORMENTS ANEW;
AND FRUSTRATOIN'S UGLY HEAD DOTH LOOM,
THRICE LARGER THAN LIFE, AS COLD AS WINTER'S DEW.
AND ALL IS HOPELESS, MISERABLE, GLOOM.
A THOUSAND TIMES SOUGHT I, THE SPHINX OF LIFE TO
SLAY.
BUT NEVER STRUCK A SINGLE BLOW. I FAILED AGAIN
TODAY.

Prince John Chaber

ECSTASY IN LOVE

MY HEART REJOICES, WHENE'ER I CHANCE TO SEE,
THAT FAIR YOUNG BEAUTY ON THE HILL.
MY SPIRIT FROLICS, MY LIFE IS FULL.
AND ALL IS JOY AND HOPE AND ECSTASY.
HER EYES SPARKLE LIKE THE GOLDEN SUNLIGHT,
UPON THE CRYSTAL WAVES BELOW.
HER HAIR IS SOFT AND SHINING BRIGHT,
LIKE SUMMER BROWN LEAVES IN THE MORNING DEW.
I CANNOT CHECK, NOR DO I CARE TO DRY,
THE LOVE SPRING FLOWING FROM MY O'ER FILLED HEART,
I CANNOT OWN, OR DARE I EVEN TRY
TO CALL HER MINE, OR MAKE HER MY SWEETHEART.
BUT WHERE LOVE ABOUNDS, THERE MUST AWAYS BE,
SOME LITTLE WISP OF JOY, WHATEVER ITS PAUCITY.

Prince John Chaber

16

LOVE'S TREASURE

AND THUS, ONCE MORE, FATE HATH A VICTIM FOUND
IN ME, A READY SLAVE OF LOVE'S LONG BEATEN TRACK.
ONCE MORE, THERE'S LIGHT. BUT ALL WILL SOON BE
BLACK;
AND MISERABLE, BROKEN, TORN, I LOOK AROUND
TO FIND THAT LOVE'S A SPHINX, AN IMPOSSIBLE THING,
THAT TORMENTS THE SOUL WHEN IT IS WONT TO REST.
TO FEEL THE PANGS OF DESIRE DISSOLVE TO NOTHING,
TO LEAVE EMPTINESS IN A ONCE HOPEFUL BREAST.
BUT CAN I DARE TO MISS E'EN THE TINIEST CHANCE
TO CONQUER ILLUSORY LOVE AT LAST?
PERCHANCE THERE LIES IN A LITTLE DISTANCE,
A FITTING TRIBUTE TO A HOPELESS PAST.
LOVE'S HIDDEN TREASURES TO ALL THE WORLD'S A PREY.
THE HUNTER AND THE HUNTED MUST, COME FACE TO
FACE SOME DAY.

Prince John Chaber

SWEET DREAMS

EACH NIGHT I SLEEP, I DREAM OF YOU, MY LOVE.
ALL PLEASANT DREAMS AND TRUE.
EACH MORNING I WOULD THINK OF YOU,
AND SEND A PRAYER TO YOU, WITH THE ANGELS ABOVE.
AND WHEN ANOTHER NIGHT IS COME,
AND I LAY ME DOWN TO SLEEP,
I WOULD DREAM I SEE AN ANGEL FORM,
WATCHING O'ER YOU WHILE YOU SLEEP.
THEN I WOULD SLEEP; BUT IN MY REPOSE,
I WOULD ONCE MORE DREAM OF YOU.
AND SNUGLY I WOULD STEAL BESIDE YOU CLOSE,
TO SHARE YOUR WARM BED OF SLUMBER TOO.
BUT SOON THE MORNING COMES, AND TAKES ME WOEFULLY
BACK TO THE WORLD OF GRIM REALITY.

Prince John Chaber

LOVE'S ENCHANTMENT

LIKE A ROSEBUD KISSED BY THE GOLDEN SUNLIGHT,
MY HEART IS OPENING OUT TO YOU, MY LOVE;
AS WIDE AS THE HEAVENS, WAY UP ABOVE
THE HILLS, THE MOUNTAINS AND THE HIGHEST HEIGHTS.
ENCHANTMENT AND DELIGHT ABUNDANTLY PREVAIL.
MY SOUL IS FILLED WITH SWEETENED THOUGHTS OF YOU.
BUT ALAS, YOU KNOW NOT WHAT ECSTASY I FEEL!
WHAT BOUNDLESS GIFTS OF JOY I KNOW.
IF FATE COULD BE BUT PLANNING STILL,
MORE JOYOUS JOYS THAN THESE,
THEN LET IT BE HER SPECIAL WILL,
TO SEND YOU TO ME WHENE'ER SHE PLEASE.
MAY THE DAY BE NEAR WHEN YOU'LL BE MINE,
FOREVER MORE TO REIGN MY DARLING, QUEEN.

Prince John Chaber

NOCTURNAL LOVE

EACH TIME I KISS YOU MY SWEETHEART,
A THOUSAND GOLDEN HARPS DOTH SING.
AND LITTLE FAIRIES, GAILY FROLICKING,
THE SWEETEST SONGS OF LOVE IMPART.
EACH TIME I KISS YOU MY DARLING,
AND LOVE'S GAY ENCHANTMENT THRILLS ME,
THE COCK CROWS AND TELLS ME I AM DREAMING,
OF A LOVE THAT NEVER WILL BE.
MY DAYS GROW LONG AND EMPTY,
BUT THEN, I EAGERLY WAIT FOR THE NIGHT,
WHEN YOU AND I WILL ONCE MORE FONDLY,
SHARE SWEET DREAMS OF RAPTUROUS DELIGHT.
SWEET DREAMS, MY LOVE, MAY THERE EVER BE,
TO IGNITE OUR NOCTURNAL ECSTASY.

Prince John Chaber

RHAPSODY IN BLUE

WITHIN ME LIES A TORTURED SOUL,
IMPRISONED IN A CAGE,
OF LOVE. IN SOLITARY BONDAGE;
SCREAMING MADLY, BUT NO ONE WILL,
TO MY RESCUE DARE TO COME.
I MUST TRAVAIL IN MISERY,
EVEN TO THE EDGE OF DOOM.
NO ONE WILL RENDER ME MERCY.
FORBIDDEN LOVE, RELENTLESS LOVE,
TORMENTS MY SOUL BY NIGHT AND DAY.
MY HEART'S A RESTLESS HEAVING ALCOVE,
CANNOT LOCK MY GRIEF AWAY.
OH MAY FATE A FRESH SHOWER IMPART,
UPON THE FLAMES OF LOVE THAT BURN WITHIN MY
HEART.

Prince John Chaber

LOST LOVE

IN DEEP DESPAIR MY HEART YEARNS FOR YOU,
MY LOVE. I CANNOT BEAR TO THINK,
YOU ARE FOREVER GONE AND THE LAST LINK
OF OUR LOVE, NOW LIES TORN ASUNDER.
WHY HAVEN'T YOU WRITTEN FOR SO LONG?
AND WHY DO THE STARS NO LONGER SHINE?
WHY CAN'T YOUR LOVE BE FOREVER MINE?
YOU SAID, MY LOVE, YOU'LL LOVE ME ALWAYS,
THAT OUR LOVE WOULD ENDURE FOR EVERMORE.
BUT HOW THESE COLDER DARKER DAYS,
HAVE DIMMED THE JOYS WE KNEW BEFORE.
OH COME, MY LOVE, LET US EMBRACE AGAIN;
AND LET OUR HEARTS SING LOVE'S GLAD REFRAIN.

Prince John Chaber

PERFIDY

LIKE A METEORITE FALLING FROM THE SKY,
IN A THOUSAND GLITTERING RAYS.
LIKE A MILLION GOLDEN SUMMER DAYS,
IN ALL THEIR ILLUMINED MAJESTY.
YOUR WORDS BROUGHT GLADNESS TO MY EAR,
AND BANISHED ALL MY MISERY.
YOUR WHISPERS TOUCHED MY DEEP DESPAIR,
AND FILLED MY HEART WITH ECSTASY.
BUT ALAS, HOW COULD I ONLY KNOW,
YOU REALLY MEANT TO TEASE?
THAT YOUR WORDS OF LOVE WERE MEANT TO SHOW
YOUR OWN CONTENT-FILLED EASE?
STILL, IF YOU'RE HAPPY, I'LL GLADLY BE,
CONTENT TO SPEND MY LIFE IN HOPELESS MISERY.

Prince John Chaber

YOUNG LOVE

WHEN IN THE FLOWER OF MY YOUTH,
I DRANK LIFE'S NECTAR SWEET;
AND ALL THE WORLD LAY AT MY FEET;
AND KISSED A GIRL FULL ON THE MOUTH.
MY SPIRIT FLEW LIKE FEATHERS THEN,
THAT'S A LADEN VESSEL NOW;
AND SCARCE CAN I REMEMBER WHEN,
A CARE WAS ON MY BROW.
BUT NOW THE STRAINS OF LIFE PREVAIL,
AND WORRIES DAILY COME.
AND MYRAID PAINS MY SOUL ASSAIL,
AND LIFE'S A BED OF GLOOM.
BUT BETTER THE MEMORIES OF A GLORIOUS YESTERYEAR,
THAN AN EPITAPH READING, "HE LIES HERE."

Prince John Chaber

TEMPTRESS

LOVER OR TEMPTRESS?
OH, PRAY TELL ME!
JUST WHO IS SHE,
WHO MAKES ME FEEL SO HELPLESS?
BUT COULD IT BE ME?
LONG BECALMED, AND NOW,
THAT ONCE RESTLESS SEA,
HAS STIRRED AGAIN SOMEHOW?
I VOWED THAT NE'ER WOULD I AGAIN,
WALK ALONG THAT THORNY PATH,
BESTREWN WITH BITTERNESS AND PAIN,
AND TEARY DAYS AND SLEEPLESS NIGHTS.
YET PASSIONS KINDLED WILL NOT DIE,
TILL FED BY LOVE'S CONSUMING ECSTASY.

Prince John Chaber

TO SYLVIA

SYLVIA, SYLVIA, OH, HOW THE SOUND OF YOUR NAME,
THE MEMORIES THAT IT BRINGS TO ME,
THE JOYS UNSPEAKBLE, THE ENDLESS ECSTASY,
KINDLES WITHIN MY HEART AN UNQUENCHABLE FLAME!
BUT FATE HATH FROM THE START DECREED,
THAT HEEDLESS OF HOW MUCH WE STROVE,
OUR CAPTIVE HEARTS CAN NE'ER BE FREED,
NOR LOOSE OUR BONDS, OR LOVE APPROVE.
AS THE LAW OF THE MEDES AND PERSIANS,
THAT ALTERS NOT THOUGH HELL MAY FREEZE,
OUR LOVE'S BEEN BECALMED LIKE GALLEONS,
IN A DEAD SEA WATCH WITHOUT A BREEZE.
OH MAY THE NORTH WIND BLOW ALONG THE SHORE,
AND SET OUR SHIPWRECKD LIVES ASTIR ONCE MORE.

Prince John Chaber

ENDLESS LOVE

WHEN OFT I THINK OF LOVE, I THINK OF YOU.
HOW LOVE, LIKE A SEED E'EN HAPLY SEWN,
WILL GERMINATE, AND SOON, FULL GROWN,
BEAR SOME SWEET FRUIT FOR LOVERS TRUE.
OH NO. LOVE NEED NOT SPRING FROM PASSION'S FLAME,
OR HEARTS DRIVEN WILDLY BY DESIRE.
FOR IT WILL OFTTIMES IGNITE JUST THE SAME,
AS THE TINIEST SPARK CAN LIGHT THE BIGGEST FIRE.
OUR LOVE AT FIRST WAS NOTHING MORE,
THAN THE TINIEST SEEDLING AND THEN A FLOWER.
BUT AS IT GREW, WITH EACH PASSING YEAR,
BECAME A TREE SO STRONG, IT WOULD LIVE FOREVER.
AND THEN ALAS, ONE DAY, THAT GREAT TREE DIED,
BUT ITS ROOTS, ALIVE BENEATH THE SOIL, RESIDE.

Prince John Chaber

AN ANATOMY OF LOVE

LOVE IS NOT FOR THE FAINT OF HEART,
IT CAN SCARCELY BE DENIED.
LOVE IS LIKE A RUSHING TIDE,
THAT CAN REND TWO STURDY HEARTS APART.
LOVE IS NOT A BED OF ROSES,
IT IS OFTEN APTLY SAID.
FOR THE HEARTACHES IT IMPOSES,
CAN MAKE A FEATHER SEEM AS LEAD.
LOVE IS NOT FOR HEROES EITHER.
IT'S A TENDER PRECIOUS THING,
THAT WILL PERISH IN THE WINTER,
OF A WAR BEGUN IN SPRING.
LOVE IS FOR LOVERS STRONG AND TRUE.
THE POTION OF THE AGES, ITS FOR ME AND YOU.

Prince John Chaber

MY TWO LOVES

MY TWO LOVES THE ONLY EARTHLY MEASURE,
THAT KEEPS MY HEART FROM BREAKING.
THE ONE'S MY LORD THE HEAVENLY KING
THE OTHER THE WIFE I TRULY TREASURE.
LIKE A BIRD TRAPPED IN A DINGY CAGE,
I AM FED FROM EARTH AND HEAVEN.
BY MY GOD IN WHOM I DO BELIEVE
BY THE WOMAN HE HAS GIVEN.
I DO NOT GRIEVE, I'M NOT ALONE,
THOUGH MY SOUL IS SICK WITH CARE.
A MANSION IN HEAVEN IS MY FINAL HOME,
AND GOD IS WITH ME HERE.
MY NAME IS WRITTEN IN THE BOOK OF LIFE,
AND BESIDE MY OWN, THAT OF MY WIFE.

Prince John Chaber

IMPRISONED SOUL

WHAT CAN UPLIFT A SPIRIT PRESSED?
BENEATH A LOAD OF CARE AND SHAME.
OR DULL THE BURNING SEARING FLAME?
OF SOULS IMPRISONED AND DISTRESSED.
OR SPAN THE GULF TWIXT LOFTY RANK,
AND ABYSMAL, CATASTROPHIC, FALL?
OR KNOW THE PAIN OF PRIDE NOW SANK,
BENEATH THE DEPTHS OF FATE'S RECALL?
WHAT OPIATES CAN MERE WORDS PROVIDE
OR FRIENDLY SMILES AVAIL?
WHEN FORTUNE'S WICKED HAND DIVIDE,
THE REASON FROM THE WILL?
IF FORTUNE'S A GODDESS, THEN LET HER BE,
CAST HEADLONG 'NEATH THE BRINY SEA.

Prince John Chaber

LOVE'S MEMORIES

WHEN IN THE WAKE OF THOUGHTS I SPENT,
ON FRUITLESS FANCIED FLIGHTS.
ON DREAMS THAT BELONG BUT TO THE NIGHT,
AND MY RESTLESS HEART FINDS NO CONTENT,
WHEN VISIONS OF YOU, FORLORN AND SAD,
COME FLOODING O'ER MY MIND,
I CRAVE THE LOVE WE ONCE HAD.
THE LOVE I HAPLESS LEFT BEHIND.
AND CAN THERE BE MORE BITTER CUP?
THAN A LOVERS HEART WHEN LONELY?
TO MOPE O'ER THE WINE HE CANNOT SUP?
AND VAIN ILLUSORY VAPORS ONLY?
AND YET, ALAS, LOVE'S MEMORIES HAUNT ME STILL.
THE CUPS' NOW EMPTY, TIME ALONE CAN FILL.

Prince John Chaber

NOCTURNE

WHEN IN NOCTURNAL'S ENDLESS SOLITUDE I SIGH,
AND MY HEART IN RESTLESS SHIFTS, DRIFTS TO AND FRO,
WHEN I'M SO DRAINED, I FEEL AS IF I WOULD DIE,
BECAUSE THE PAIN OF LONELINESS GRIPS ME IN THE NIGHT.
THEN WOULD I PRAY FOR SLEEP'S BEGUILING CALM,
WHEN SUPER-EGO, EGO, ID, AS IS THEIR WONT,
WOULD VAINLY VIE FOR SOME HYPNOTIC BALM
TO SATE THE PSYCHE AND MAKE THE SOUL RELENT.
BUT LIKE MYRAID EPHEMERAE, FLIRTING WITH THE LIGHT,
SLEEP FLITS BY AND IN A MOMENT SOON IS GONE.
AND ALL ALONE, IN ANOTHER SLEEPLESS PLIGHT,
I COUNT EACH MOMENT TOSSED, FROM DUSK TO DAWN.
BUT AS THE SUNLIGHT GREETS THE DEW ON MY WINDOW SILL,
I'M REMINDED THERE'LL BE OTHER SLEEPLESS NIGHTS AS WELL.

Prince John Chaber

TO ELSA

BUT FOR YOU, MY LOVE, LIFE WOULD DOUBTLES CEASE
TO BE,
AND THIS WORLDLY PAIN WOULD BE LONG PAST,
WERE IT NOT FOR THE UNFORGETTABLY PRECIOUS
THOUGHT,
OF DAYS ONCE FILLED WITH SWEETEST ECSTASY.
WHAT CAN I SAY? I LOVE YOU MORE THAN LIFE ITSELF;
BUT WHAT IS LIFE, WITHOUT THE ONE YOU LOVE?
AND WHAT BALM'S ENOUGH TO GIVE FOR LOVER'S GRIEF,
SAVE THE THOUGHT THAT LOVE'S SUFFICIENT UNTO
LOVE?
OH, IF WE COULD BUT CROSS THAT AWFUL BRIDGE,
WHAT JOYOUS DAYS AND NIGHTS THERE'D BE?
WHEN WE WOULD THEN BE LOST IN LOVE FOREVER,
RAPTUROUSLY ENTWINED IN A BLISSFUL JUBILEE.
OH, MAY LOVE'S FOUNTAIN NEVER CEASE TO FLOW.
FOR TOGETHER AGAIN, OUR HEARTS WILL BE AGLOW.

Prince John Chaber

THE CORDS OF LOVE

CAN LOVERS HEATS STILL BEAT AS ONE?
WHEN COLD, STEELY, WALLS DIVIDE US?
AND, WOUNDED BY MEAN, FIERY, DARTS,
THUS THEY'RE LEFT TO GRIEVE ALONE?
YET LOVE'S GOLDEN TREAD WILL HOLD,
WHATEVER THE WEIGHT OR STRESS.
FOR, AS TIME CANNOT DECAY THE GOLD,
THAT'S LAID UP IN A TREASURE CHESS,
SO, TRUE LOVERS HEARTS TIME WILL SEAL,
AGAINST COLD, DARK, DAYS OF WINTER.
TO KEEP LOVE'S FLAME ALIVE UNTIL,
THE WARMER, BRIGHER, RAYS OF SUMMER.
FOR THE CORDS OF LOVE'S A GOLDEN THREAD.
IT WIL SURVIVE THE CARE WORN DAYS AHEAD.

Prince John Chaber

TO JARES

WHEN FROM THE DEPTH OF LOVE CONFINED,
SAD, BITTER, TEARS DOTH FLOW.
AND PAIN I PRAY YOU'LL NEVER KNOW,
MY LONELINESS BRINGS TO MIND
I THINK OF YOU MY LITTLE FLOWER;
AND DULLS MY PAIN AWHILE.
BUT SOON THERE SPRINGS ANOTHER SHOWER,
AND DROWNS WHAT WAS A SMILE.
BUT 'TIS A JOY YOU DO NOT KNOW,
WHAT GRIEF I SUFFER HERE.
BUT IF MY ANGEL'S HEART DOTH GLOW,
MY SORROWS I CAN BEAR.
SO FARE THEE WELL, MY LITTLE MAN,
I'LL SEE YOU SOON, OR HOPE I CAN.

Prince John Chaber

TO DEVRES

OH, MY SON, MY LIFE, MY PRIDE, MY JOY.
WHAT MEASURELESS GRIEF I FEEL FOR YOU!
FOR WHAT CAN CHEER A HEART THAT BEATS SO TRUE?
WHAT CAN FILL THE VOID LEFT BY YOU MY BOY?
IF TEARS COULD WASH AWAY THE BITTER PAIN,
THEN TEARS AND TEARS AGAIN I'LL FREELY SHED.
BUT ALL THE TEARS WOULD SADLY BE IN VAIN,
EVEN THOUGH I WEEP AN OCEAN, OR TILL I'M DEAD.
BUT THERE'S ONE WHO STILL CAN STRENGTHEN,
CHEERLESS HEARTS, THOUGH FRAIL AND WEAK.
AND MY FAITH IN HIM CAN NEVER BE SHAKEN
AS FAITHFULLY HIS FACE I HUMBLY SEEK.
I LOVE YOU, DEVRES, AND NOTHING CAN ERASE,
THE BOND BETWIXT US, NOR CAN TAKE ITS PLACE.

Prince John Chaber

TO SONJA

WHEN IN THE WAKE OF DAYS LONG SPENT,
THE PAIN OF CRUEL FATE TRANSFORM,
TWO HAPPY LIVES, AND DREARY DOOM,
ENTOMB OUR SAD SPIRITS IN TORMENT.
I THINK OF THOSE HAPPY DAYS, WHEN WE,
WERE ALL ALONE AND THE MANY GAMES WE PLAY.
AND FUN AND LAUGHTER, MIRTH AND JOLLITY,
SURROUND US, THROUGHOUT THE LIVE LONG DAY.
OBLIVIOUS WERE WE THEN, THAT ALL TOO SOON,
OUR HAPPY DAYS WOULD QUICKLY FLY AWAY,
AND SAD, BROKEN, MIRTHLESS AND FORLORN,
WE WOULD FEAR THE DAWN OF ANOTHER DAY.
SONJA MY LOVE, LET US IN CONSTANT HOPE REMAIN,
THAT SUNSHINE DAYS WILL WARM OUR LIVES AGAIN.

Prince John Chaber

VALENTINE EVERY DAY

LOVE IS FOR LOVERS, LOVERS SAY,
'TIS THE OPIATE OF THE SOUL.
THE PENNY TOSSED IN EVERY WISHING WELL,
FRESH FROM THE MINT SINCE CUPID'S DAY.
'TIS THE VERY FONT FOR AGED POET'S PEN,
THE FOOD OF LIFE FOR ROMANTC BARD.
IT IS A CEASELESS EFFFERVESCENT FOUNTAIN,
FLOWING EVER INWARD AND FOREVER UPWARD.
BUT VALENTINE'S IS A VERY SPECIAL LOVE,
BECAUSE ITS GOOD FOR ALL THE YEAR.
ITS FRAGRANCE SWEET AS THE EGLANTINE,
FLOATING O'ER THE FRESH SUMMER AIR.
IF EVERY DAY BE VALENTINE'S, HEARTS, KISSES, SINCERE,
LOVERS HEARTS WOULD FONDLY BEAT, ALL THROUGH
THE YEAR.

Prince John Chaber

A VALENTINE WISH

VALENTINE IS FOR LOVERS,
SO SOME PEOPLE GLIBLY SAY.
BUT EVERY DAY IS VALENTINE'S DAY,
IT'S THE LOVE POTION OF THE AGES.
THE FLAME OF LOVE IS EVERLASTING,
WHEN LIT BY TRUE DESIRE.
ITS AN INCANDESCEN ALL CONSUMING,
ETERNAL, GLOWING, DEVOURING, FIRE.
AND VALENTINE'S FOR THE YOUNG AT HEART,
TRANSCENDING TIME AND SPACE.
AND E'EN WHEN LOVERS ARE APART,
IT WILL NEVER LOSE ITS PLACE.
FOR THE FLAME OF LOVE WILL STILL BURN ON
E'EN WHEN PASSION'S EARLY FIRE IS GONE.

Prince John Chaber

LOVERS VALENTINE

WHEN TWO LOVERS HEARTS CAN BEAT AS ONE,
AND EACH TO EACH DECLARE,
A PLEDGE TO LAST ALL THROUGH THE YEAR,
AND LOVE GLOWS WARM AS THE NOONDAY SUN.
THEN NOTHING CAN THOSE HEARTS E'ER SEVER,
NO MATTER HOW LONG THEY ARE ALONE.
FOR ABSENCE OFT MAKES HEARTS GROW STRONGER,
WHEN DAYS ARE DARK AND MIRTH IS GONE.
AND WHAT BETER TIME FOR LOVERS FOND,
IN A THOUSAND SWEET WAYS TO SAY,
COME MY LOVE, LET US RENEW OUR BOND,
AND LET MELANCHOLY HASTLY FLY AWAY.
FOR VALENTINE IS NOT BUT A SINGLE DAY,
'TIS A GOLDEN STORE FOR ALL ETERNITY.

Prince John Chaber

LOVE

I VENTURE THAT, LOVE ONCE DEFINED,
IS THEN NO LONGER LOVE.
AS FREEDOM, ONCE IT IS CONFINED,
IS NO LONGER FREEDOM, SO IS LOVE.
"THOUGH LOVE IS KIND AND SUFFERS LONG,"
"THOUGH LOVE IS MEEK AND DOES NO WRONG,"
"THOUGH THAN DEATH ITSELF MORE STRONG,"
YET, TO NONE OF THESE, DOTH LOVE BELONG.
LOVE IS WIDER THAN ALL THE GREAT OCEANS.
AND MUCH MORE RESTLESS THAN ALL THE SEAS.
IT TRANSCENDS ALL OUR ROMANTC NOTIONS,
IT DEFIES ALLTHE AGED PHILOSOPHIES.
FOR LOVE IS LIFE AND DEATH AND JOY AND PAIN
COMBINED.
IMMEASRABLE, BOUNDLESS, ITS BODY AND SOUL AND
MIND.

Prince John Chaber

THE LITTLE APPLE TREE

THERE WAS ONCE A LITTLE APPLE TREE,
STANDING FIRM BUT BARE.
ITS LITTLE BRANCHES SHAKILY,
BENT IN THE FROSTY AIR.

AND THEN ONE DAY THE BIG SNOW SHOWED,
AND COVERED IT ALL OVER.
HOW SAD AND WET AND COLD AND BOWED,
IT EVEN GAVE A SHIVER.

BUT THEN AT LAST THE SUNSHINE CAME
AND TINY LITTLE BUDS APPEAR
AND GREEN LEAVES ON EVERY STEM
WERE FROLICKING WITH THE RESTLESS AIR.

ALL DECKED WITH PRETTY FLOWERS NOW,
IT BECKONED EVERY BEE
TO TASTE SWEET NECTAR ON EACH BOW
AS THEY FORAGED BUSILY.

AT LAST THE GOLDEN FRUIT APPEAR,
THE BRANCHES SAG AND BEND.
THE HARVEST OF ANOTHER YEAR,
WILL MARK THE SUMMER'S END.

Prince John Chaber

TO MOTHER WITH LOVE

THANKS TO YOU, MY MOTHER,
FOR BEING ALWAYS THERE FOR ME.
IN A WAY LIKE NO OTHER,
HOWEVER CLOSE, COULD EVER BE.

AMONG MY EARLIEST MEMORIES,
WAS MY MOTHER'S TENDER CARE.
IN A HUNDRED DIFFERENT WAYS
YOU WERE ALWAYS, OH, SO DEAR.

I REMEMBER WHEN THE FEVER STRUCK,
WHEN I WAS SIX OR SEVEN.
AND DELIRIUM NEAR MY SENSES TOOK,
AND SENT ME UP TO HEAVEN.

OH, I REMEMBER SO MANY THINGS,
I DIDN'T THEN UNDERSTAND.
BUT THERE BESIDE MY RAMBLINGS
YOU SAT AND HELD MY HAND.

THE LESSONS YOU EARLY INCULCATE,
THE DO'S AND DONT'S OF LIFE.
THOSE ARE THE THINGS I APPRECIATE,
THE SINE QUA NON OF MY BELIEF.

AND THOUGH OFT, THE LESSONS TAUGHT,
WERE REINFORED WITH THE STRAP,
THEY TAUGHT ME EARLY HOW I OUGHT,
TO WALK UPRIGHT AND KEEP IN STEP.

I REMEMBER WELL ADOLESCENT YEARS,
AND THE MANY VICISSTITUDES OF LFE,
SAD MOMENTS WHEN A MOTHER'S TEARS,
PAID THE PRICE FOR BOYHOOD MISHCHIEF.

WASTE NOT, WANT NOT, YOU WOULD SAY,
AND LET TRUTH ALWAYS BE YOUR GUIDE.
AND MAKE HAY WHILE YET ITS DAY,
AND NEVER, NEVER WALK, BY SATAN'S SIDE.

THEN I ARRIVED AT MANHOOD,
AND OFTTIMES HARDSHIPS WOULD ASSAIL.
BUT AT THOSE TIMES I ALWAYS WOULD,
LET THOSE LESSONS TAUGHT PREVAIL.

AND WHEN THE DARKEST HOUR CAME,
AND FAME AND FORTUNE FAILED ME,
THERE WAS MY MOTHER, JUST THE SAME,
WITH HER TENDER ARMS AROUND ME.

MERE WORDS ARE BUT INADEQUATE,
TO EXPRESS MY LOVE FOR YOU.
BUT I KNOW OF NO OTHER MEDIATE,
NOTHING ELSE THAT I CAN DO.

SAVE TO SAY A LITTLE PRAYER,
EACH NIGHT I SEEK MY BED.
AND PRAY THE LORD, WITH HEART SINCERE,
THAT YOU MAY BE SPIRIT LED.

I LOVE YOU, MOTHER DEAR,
MAY GOD'S RICHEST BLESSINGS BE,
ALWAYS WITH YOU, FAR OR NEAR,
NOW AND THROUGH ALL ETERNITY.

Prince John Chaber

ODE TO MY ENEMIES

I CALL YOU FRIEND, NO MATTER WHAT,
YOU SAY OR THINK OF ME.
FOR I HAVE NO ROOM WITHIN MY HEART,
FOR SPITEFUL HATE OR ENMITY.

IF YOU HATE ME FOR SOME WRONG,
YOU THINK I'VE DONE TO YOU,
DO FORGIVE, AND SEE E'ER LONG,
YOUR HEART WILL LOVE ME TOO.

AND IF YOU FIND THIS HARD TO DO,
I URGE YOU, COME WHAT MAY,
AND NOT BECAUSE I ASK YOU TO
BUT BROTHER, YOU NEED TO PRAY.

I HAVE NO ENEMIES THAT I KNOW,
FOR I PRAY GOD EVERY DAY.
FORGIVE AND LET FORGIVENESS SHOW,
IN THE LIVES OF MEN IN EVERY WAY.

FOR HATE IS LIKE A CANCEROUS GROWTH,
EATING AWAY AT THE SOULS OF MEN.
BEREFTING THEM OF ALL MORAL WORTH,
AS USELESS AS AN INK-LESS PEN.

HOW CAN WE SAY FORGIVE US LORD,
WHEN OUR HEARTS, AS HARD AS STONE,
POISONED WITH HATE, THE LIVING WORD,
CANNOT NEW LIFE GIVE, OUR SIN ATONE?

SO LET THE HATCHET BE, NOW BURIED HERE,
AND LET PEACE AND LOVE PREVAIL.
OUR PRAYERS CANNOT BE HEARD UP THERE,
IF INIQUITY IN OUR HEARTS DOTH DWELL.

GOD CALLS ALL MEN TO LIVE IN PEACE,
THAT IS WHY HE CAME TO EARTH.
THAT STRIFE AND RANCOR MAY CEASE,
AND SHARE THE FULNESS OF HIS BIRTH.

FORGIVE, O MY BROTHER,
E'ER THE SETTING SUN,
SIGNALS THAT THE DAY IS OVER
OR THE COURSE OF LIFE BE RUN.

Prince John Chaber

TO MY FRIENDS

TO ALL THOSE WHO REMAIN MY FRIENDS,
WHO STOOD THROUGH THICK AND THIN,
AND LOVED ME WHEN THE WICKED FIENDS,
JAWS AGAPE, OPENED WIDE TO SWALLOW IN.

TO YOU I SAY, I LOVE YOU TOO,
FOR LOVE DOES NOT DECLINE,
LOVE CHANGETH NOT, AND SO I KNOW,
JUST WHO ARE FRIENDS OF MINE.

I CAN BUT THANK YOU FROM MY HEART,
AND WHAT MORE COULD I GIVE?
WHAT MORE PRECIOUS THAN THE THOUGHT?
OF UNFEIGNED THANKFULNESS IN LOVE.

TO YOU, I SAY, YOUR GOOD REWARD,
YOU'LL RECEIVE SEVENTY TIMES SEVEN.
AS YOUR SPIRITS SOAR, EVER UPWARD,
AND YOU ARRIVE AT LAST IN HEAVEN.

MAY GOD'S RICHEST BLESSINGS,
FILL YOUR KIND HEARTS AND MIND.
AND MAY ALL YOUR FONDEST LONGINGS,
IN HEAVEN A PLACE DOTH FIND.

AND KNOW FOR SURE GOD IS WATCHING.
ALL OUR WORDS AND ACTIONS HERE.
HE'S EVER PRESENT EVER WAITING,
TO MEET HIS LOVE ONES IN THE AIR.

Prince John Chaber

SAINT WHO?

BLARNEY, KILARNEY,
WHAT DO THEY MEAN?
WHY? DO THEY DECRY?
MY EMERALD QUEEN?
OR CAN A GEM SO PRECIOIUS RARE,
BE TARNISHED BY IRELAND'S SULTRY AIR?
BUNKUM, O'RILEY
CAN THESE BE,
ALIENS HAPLY
FORCED ON ME?
NOT WELCOMED THEN NOR HONORED NOW,
BUT ETCHD FOREVER ON MY BROW?
DALEY, O'GARRO,
WHAT'S YOUR NAME,
JOY OR SORROW,
PRIDE OR SHAME?
IS THERE NO REMEDY, NO OPIATE
TO BREAK THE CHAINS OR DULL THE HURT?
PATRICK, SAINT
OR, SINNER HE?
DOES IT MATTER WHAT?
'TIS ALL THE SAME TO ME.
IS THERE NO NAME WHOSE BLOOD I BEAR
OR WERE THEY MURDERED EVERYWHERE?

Elsa Greenaway Weekes

A DIRGE

OH LAND OF OUR FOREFATHERS TOLD,
IN ENDLESS TALES OF WOE,
OF DEEDS TOO TERRIBLE TO BEHOLD
IN DAYS OF LONG AGO.

THE BEATINGS AND THE WHIPPINGS SORE,
THE GRINDING AT THE MILL
THE SUNSTROKE AND THE FOODLESS STORE
THE EVER EMPTY WELL.

LET US FORGET THOSE AWFUL DAYS,
LET US BE MEN AND LIVE
LET HATE'S ANGRY TWISTED SEEDS
NOT LIVE IN THE WEST INDIES.

LET UNITY BE OUR WATCHWORD,
AND PROGRESS BE OUR GUIDE.
LET NOT REVENGE'S BLOODY SWORD
PIERCE OUR CHILDREN'S SIDE.

LET EVERY ONE OF US BE HAPPY
THAT OUR FOREBEARS MADE US FREE.
LET NOT THE CRUEL GHOST OF TYRANNY,
WALK THE SANDS OF THE CARIBBEE.

Prince John Chaber

EMERALD SERENADE

OH, LAND OF MY BIRTH,
OH, BRIGHT MORNING STAR.
A FOUNTAIN OF MIRTH,
EMERALD STILL YOU ARE.
THOUGH YEARS ROLL AWAY
FOREVER, I'LL SAY,
OH MONTSERRAT, I LOVE YOU.

YOUR MOUNTAINS SO GREEN,
YOUR DAYS ARE SO FAIR.
YOUR VALLEYS SERENE,
YOUR WATERS SO CLEAR.
THOUGH YEARS ROLL AWAY,
FOREVER, I'LL SAY,
OH MONTSERRAT, I LOVE YOU.

I JOURNEY NEAR AND FAR,
TO LANDS FAR AND WIDE.
BUT NO OTHER COMPARE,
TO THE CHARM YOU PROVIDE.
THOUGH YEARS ROLL AWAY,
FOREVER, I'LL SAY,
OH, MONTSERRAT, I LOVE YOU.

WHEN TIME SHALL BE AT HAND,
AND LIFE SHALL BE NO MORE,
LET ME REST IN THE SAND,
OF YOUR RICH VERDANT SHORE.
THOUGH YEARS ROLL AWAY,
FOREVER, I'LL SAY,
OH MONTSERRAT, I LOVE YOU.

Prince John Chaber

THE TWINS

BEDUMBED WAS I, WHEN NATURE SAID,
YOUR LOINS SHALL ONCE MORE BEAR.
BUT TWO PLUS ONE ARE THREE, I CRIED,
NO SAID SHE, TWO PLUS TWO ARE FOUR.

DUMBFOUNDED I, THE MEDICS SOUGHT,
THE ORACLE TO CONFOUND.
BUT ALL MY PROTESTS WERE AT NOUGHT,
"TWINS," SAID THE ULTRA SOUND,

THEN SOUGHT I GOD, REPRIEVE TO GIVE,
AND PRAYED I DID TILL SORE.
"PETITION DENIED! TRUST AND BELIEVE,
THE VERDICT STANDS, TWO MORE!"

ABORTION WAS NO OPTION. FOR,
TO DO SO, WOULD BE TO MURDER.
AND WHAT COULD I DO, BUT PONDER?
SINCE I DID NOT WANT TO BE A KILLER.

FOR EACH TINY THROB OF LIFE,
IS COVERED BY THE BLOOD.
AND AT OUR HANDS, HE WILL REQUIRE
THE BLOOD OF MAN, 'TIS IN HIS WORD.

SO DAUNTED I, IN HUMBLE MIEN,
RESOLVED TO DO THE MASTER'S WILL.
WAS PRESENT WHEN IN CRUSHIG PAIN,
CAME FORTH TWO MORE MOUTHS TO FILL.

MINDFUL OF MY INITIAL PRAYERS,
MY MIND NOW QUESTIONED, COULD THERE BE?
AS PAY BACK FOR MY WAYWARD WAYS,
SOME TERRIBLE DEFORMITY?

APPREHENSIVELY, I HASTE TO SCAN,
FACE, HANDS, FEET, TOES AND ALL,
BEING MOST ANXIOUS TO DETERMINE,
IF FATE SMILED ON ME, MY SINS WITHAL.

RELIEVED I WAS, FOR ALL WAS WELL,
THE DELIVERY WAS SAFE AND SOUND.
AND SO, AS FAR AS I COULD TELL,
THEY WERE THE HANDSOMEST BOYS AROUND.

RODNEY AND RILEY ARE THEIR NAMES,
AND NOW, I AM AS PLEASE AS PIE.
FOR GOD IS GOOD AND HE PROVIDES
I CANNOT PRETEND OR SPEAK A LIE.

NOW AT THREE MONTHS, HOW THEY GROW,
THEY GURGLE AND SMILE AND KICK AND PLAY,
THOUGH WHAT THEY SAY, I DO NOT KNOW,
I'M JUST GLAD TO SEE THEM ACT THAT WAY.

AND SOON THEY'LL CREEP AND LEARN TO WALK,
AND SOON WILL LEARN A THOUSAND THINGS.
AND DELIGHT US ALL WHEN THEY CAN TALK,
AND MAKE HAPPY SOUNDS AND MIMICKINGS.

AND VERY SOON THEY'LL UNDERSTAND,
SOME SIMPLE WORDS AND PHRASES.
I'LL TELL THEM OF THE MASTER AND,
TEACH THEM WELL TO SING HIS PRAISES.

I'LL TELL THEM GOD IS WONDERFUL,
BECAUSE HE IS A GOD OF LOVE.
I'LL TEACH THEM THAT HE'S BOUNTIFUL,
AND POINT TO HIS HEAVENLY THRONE ABOVE.

THEN, TOGETHER, WE'LL SING HIS PRAISES,
AND I'LL ALSO TEACH THEM HOW TO PRAY.
AND THAT HIS MERCY NEVER CEASES,
AND HE IS THE SAME ALWAY.

PRAISE, GLORY, LAUD AND HONOR LORD,
I'M GLAD I TOOK YOU AT YOUR WORD.
A MIGHTY FORTRESS IS OUR GOD,
OUR STRENGTH, OUR STAY, OUR SHIELD.

I THANK YOU LORD FOR GIVING ME,
SUCH PRECIOUS GIFTS AS THESE.
I PRAY THROUGH ALL ETERNITY,
YOU'LL BLESS AND KEEP THEM, PLEASE.

Prince John Chaber

ANGRY BLACK MEN

WHY ARE YOU SO ANGRY BROTHER MAN?
WHY DO YOU SHAKE WITH FURY SO?
WHY THREE HUNDRED YEARS, IN THIS FAIR LAN'
YOU'RE STILL A STRANGER, NO PLACE TO GO.

YOU SAY THE WHITE MAN TREAT YOU BAD,
YOU'RE DEPRIVED, DOWN-TRODDEN, FORLORN.
BEREFT OF THE DIGNITY YOU NEVER COULD,
ACHIEVE IN THE LAND WHERE YOU WERE BORN.

YOU STAND WITH MEN OF FAME AND STATURE.
YOU WALK HARD ROADS AND FREEDOM CRY,
BUT YOU CANNOT CHANGE HUMAN NATURE,
THOUGH YOU SWEAT AND FIGHT AND DIE.

AND WHEN REASON DID NOT WIN THE DAY,
YOU FILL YOUR HEART WITH VENGEFUL HATE.
AND THEN YOU SIT AND SEETHE AND SAY,
I TOIL IN VAIN, 'TIS BUT MY FATE.

YOU NEVER MISS THE CHANCE TO PROVE,
JUST HOW MALIGNANT YOU CAN BE.
AND THOUGH BRED TO LIVE IN LOVE AND PEACE,
YOUR HATE IS ALL THE WHITE FOLKS SEE.

COME MY BROTHER, REASON YET AHILE,
WHAT CAN HATE BEGET BUT GREATER HATE?
YOU LOOT AND ROB AND KILL AND SPOIL,
AND YET YOUR PLIGHT DOES NOT ABATE.

"BURN, LOS ANGELES, BURN," YOU CHANT,
'TIS BUT A FITTING NEMESIS YOU SAY.
"SO LET ME TAKE ALL THE LOOT I WANT,
AND LET ALL MEN REMEMVER ME THIS WAY."

"BUT ITS NOT MY FAULT," YOU HASTEN ON,
"SOCIETY MUST PAY, FOR THEY HAVE SINNED.
THE JUDICIAL SYSTEM IS NO PARAGON,
OF VIRTUE. PURE JUSTICE, IS MY DEMAND."

BUT WAIT, MY FIREND AND ANSWER THIS,
WHAT WAS THE CAUSE IN STRICKEN MIAMI?
IN THAT RUINED CITY YOU DID NOT MISS,
THE CHANCE TO SATE YOUR THIEVERY.

MARK THIS MY FRIENDS, AND MARK IT WELL,
VILLAINY WILL NOT WIN YOU WHAT YOU CRAVE.
AND IF YOU DOUBT ME, TIME ALONE WILL TELL,
YOU'LL BE TREATED MUCH AS YOU BEHAVE.

YOUR WOMEN, ONCE MONUMENTS OF YOUR RACE,
TEACHER, SOCIAL WORKER, PROVIDER, MOTHER
NOW, A PERMANENT SCOWL UPON HER FACE.
SO FULL OF HATE, SHE'S A WALKING CANCER.

HER EVERY SYLLABLE SPEAK PROFANITY AND BILE,
LIKE A VENOMOUS VIPER SPARRING FOR A FIGHT.
EVER ON THE WARPATH, SEARCHING ALL THE WHILE,
FOR SOME HAPLESS PREY, TO VENT HER SPITE.

BUT JUSTICE IS NOT A CARPENTER'S TOOL,
TO BE PASSED FROM HAND TO HAND.
THE BANE OF EVERY EMPTY-HEADED FOOL,
OR GANG OF SAVAGE LOOTING VAGABONDS.

FOR JUSTICE'S LOFTY THRONE WAS FITLY SET,
BY SINCERE, UPRIGHT, STURDY MEN OF OLD.
AGAINST THE TEST OF TIME, IT STOOD AND YET,
IT SHINES MORE BRIGHTLY THAN THE FINEST GOLD.

THROUGH STORM AND TEMPEST, FIRE AND FLOOD
THE CORNERSTONE OF OUR SOCIETY PROUDLY STAND.
AND THOUGH BETIMES ITS MARRED WITH BLOOD,
ITS STILL THE BEST THING IN THE LAND.

LET JUSTICE LIVE FOR ONE AND ALL,
FOR THOSE WHO WORK AND THOSE WHO STEAL.
LET EACH MAN ANSWER TO ITS CALL,
IF DISSATISFIED, THEN, LET HIM APPEAL.

IT IS A SYSTEM SPAWNED BY MEN 'TIS TRUE.
AND SO LIKE MEN, IT WILL FALL SHORT.
IT'S MADE FOR ALL, NOT JUST THE FEW.
ANARCHISTS SHOULD NOT TEAR IT APART.

WHY ARE YOU ANGRY, BROTHER MAN?
IS THERE FELONY ON YOUR MIND?
START BEHAVING LIKE A HUMAN.
MEN MAY LOVE YOU. FOR LOVE IS BLIND.

BUT IF PERCHANCE THEY LOVE YOU NOT,
WHAT DOES IT REALLY MATTER?
MEN'S RESPECT! THAT'S REALLY WHAT,
YOU SHOULD BE STRIVING AFTER.

BRAVE MEN LOOK NOT BACK.
THEY RISE UP WITH THE DAWN.
COWARDS SEE NOTHING BUT,
THE SHADOW OF THE SETTING SUN.

Prince John Chaber

PART II

THOUGHTS AND MEDITATIONS

MAN'S VANITY

A MOTHER'S AGONIZING GASP.
THE MIDWIFE'S HURRIED SLAP.
A BABY CRIES, AN AWFUL WAIL,
OH, WHAT IS MAN, IF MAN'S SO FRAIL?

AN INFANT IN HIS CRADLE NOW,
A FEVER BURNING ON HIS BROW.
BUT ALL THE CARE MAY NOT AVAIL.
OH, WHAT IS MAN, IF MAN'S SO FRAIL?

A TODDLER LEAVES HIS MAMA'S KNEE,
BUT OH, THERE IS TRAGEDY!
THE INFANT STEPS UPON A NAIL.
OH, WHAT IS MAN, IF MAN'S SO FRAIL?

A BIG BOY NOW, HE'S IN A GAME,
SOMEONE LETS FLY AND HE IS LAME.
BROKEN BONES? A SORRY TALE.
OH, WHAT IS MAN, IF MAN'S SO FRAIL?

"GOD BLESS YOU BOY, OH, HOW YOU SNEEZE!
YOUR CHEST IS NOW A FRANTIC WHEEZE.
TAKE THIS BOY, INHALE, INHALE!
OH, WHAT IS MAN, IF MAN'S SO FRAIL?

A YOUNG MAN IN THE ARMY STRONG,
MARCHING MERRILY ALONG.
FROM A TINY BALL OF LEAD, WILL FALL.
OH, WHAT IS MAN, IF MAN'S SO FRAIL.

A VETERAN THEN? OH, YES AN ACE,
BUT STILL HE'S LOST WITHOUT A TRACE.
HIS WIDOW NOW, DOTH WEEP AND WAIL.
OH, WHAT IS MAN, IF MAN'S SO FRAIL.

A GENERAL HE, LEADER OF MEN
BATTLES A PLENTY, THREE SCORE AND TEN.
BUT YET HE CHOKES UPON A SNAIL.
OH, WHAT IS MAN, IF MAN'S SO FRAIL.

A HUMBLE FARMER THEN, IS HE,
STRONG AND STURDY THIRTY THREE.
A SEVERED ARTERY FROM A FALL.
OH, WHAT IS MAN, IF MAN'S SO FRAIL.

A POWERFUL MAN IS HE THEY SAY,
FOR O'ER THE NATION HE HATH SWAY.
THE ASSASSIN'S DAGGERED HAND ASSAIL.
OH, WHAT IS MAN, IF MAN'S SO FRAIL?

FLAMBOYANT PRESIDENT, PEOPLE'S MAN, IS HE.
LOVED BY ALL, SENSATIONAL, A PRODIGY.
A MADMAN'S BULLET HITS THE MARK, IS SKULL.
OH, WHAT IS MAN, IF MAN'S SO FRAIL?

A KING IN REGAL GARB COMPLETE,
WITH MIGHTY BABYLON AT HIS FEET.
NOW LIKE A SWINE, EATS FROM A PAIL.
OH, WHAT IS MAN, IF MAN'S SO FRAIL.

MIGHTY CLAUDIUS IS HIS DAY,
UNWRIT THE LAW OF SANGUINITY.
BUT A LITTLE MUSHROOM CAUSED HIS FALL.
OH, WHAT IS MAN, IF MAN'S SO FRAIL?

RICHARD WAS A WARRIOR KING,
WHEN HE WAS NOT FROLICKING.
BUT FOR A FOAL WOULD GIVE HIS ALL
OH, WHAT IS MAN, IF MAN'S SO FRAIL?

THE GREATEST PROPHET, TOO, WAS JOHN.
SENT TO PREACH REPENTANCE UNTO SALVATION.
BUT AT A WENCH'S WHIM, HIS HEAD DID FALL.
OH, WHAT IS MAN, IF MAN'S SO FRAIL?

STEPHEN HAD A SAINTLY CALLING,
BUT TO SOME MEN HIS WORDS WERE GALLING.
AND DIED A WOEFUL DEATH WITHAL.
OH, WHAT IS MAN, IF MAN'S SO FRAIL?

OLD MAN SITTING IN THE PARK,
DID NOT NOTICE IT WAS DARK.
THE YOUTH WHO SLAYED HIM NOW IN JAIL.
OH, WHAT IS MAN, IF MAN'S SO FRAIL?

YOUNG MAN COMING FROM HIS JOB,
GOT LYNCHED BY A DRUNKEN MOB.
THE LAW IS SOUGHT TO NO AVAIL.
OH, WHAT IS MAN, IF MAN'S SO FRAIL?

OLD MAN LYING IN HIS BED,
FOUR SCORE AND TWENTY, HE IS DEAD.
A TEARDROP FALLS A WIDOW'S WAIL.
OH, WHAT IS MAN, IF MAN'S SO FRAIL?

YOUNG MAN PARTYING WITH HIS FRIEND,
TAKES A NEEDLE IN HIS HAND.
HIS LIFE IS NOW BEYOND THE PALE.
OH, WHAT IS MAN, IF MAN'S SO FRAIL.

YOUNG MAN, FULL OF LIFE AND VERVE,
VIRUS NOW INFECTING EVERY NERVE.
NO LONGER FLIES HE WITH THE BALL.
OH, WHAT IS MAN, IF MAN'S SO FRAIL?

CHAMPION OF THE WORLD IS HE,
VICTIM OF FEMININE CALUMNY.
THE HAMMER FALLS HE'S OFF TO JAIL,
OH, WHAT IS MAN, IF MAN'S SO FRAIL?

JURIST. WISE AND ABLE MAN, IS HE,
STRAIGHT AS THE STATUE OF LIBERTY.
PRESUMPTUOUS MAID, DOTH HE ASSAIL,
OH, WHAT IS MAN IF MAN'S SO FRAIL?

OLD WOMAN, MOTHER OF THE MAN,
FIVE SCORE AND TEN, BARELY HUMAN.
FOR NOW SHE'S BUT AN EMPTY SHELL
OH, WHAT IS MAN? YES, MAN IS FRAIL.

RICH MAN, POOR MAN, YOUNG OR OLD,
STRONG MAN WEAK MAN, WOMAN CHILD,
ALL IS VANITY. 'TIS THE MASTER'S WILL.
MAN IS GRASS. HE'S VANITY AND OH, SO FRAIL.

Prince John Chaber

YESTERDAY, TODAY, TOMORROW

YESTERDAY, I was a child,
Drooling on my mother's lap.
TODAY, I am a man,
Unfulfilled, savage, wild!
TOMORROW, I will be a child,
Drowning in my own sap.

YESTERDAY, I was lonely,
Looking for the companion of my life.
TODAY, I am a husband.
Lord of my life, a man of destiny.
TOMORROW, I shall be lonely.
Looking for another wife.

YESTERDAY, I was a hater,
Sipping the bitter cup of malignancy.
TODAY, I am a lover,
Drinking, from a cup of sweet nectar.
TOMORROW, I will be a hater,
Holding an empty cup of despondency.

YESTERDAY, I was a pauper,
Dreaming of a pot of gold.
TODAY, I am a rich man,
Millions piling high in my coffer.
TOMORROW, I will be a pauper,
Saying all that glitters is not gold.

YESTERDAY, I was a weak man,
Envying all who seemed strong.
TODAY, I am a strong man,
Building muscles, pumping iron.
TOMORROW, I will be a weakling,
Hating all who seemeth strong.

YESTERDAY, I was a hungry soul,
Searching hard for food and shelter.
TODAY, I am a gourmet.
Drinking fine wines, eating filet sole.
TOMORROW, I will again be a hungry fool,
Having not e'en a cup of water.

YESTERDAY, I was a dreamer,
Having grand visions of political power.
TODAY, I am President of a great nation,
Holding sway o'er affairs of many.
TOMORROW, I will be an exile,
Reminiscing sadly about yesteryear.

YESTERDAY, I was a social outcast,
Unknown, unrecognized by men.
TODAY, I am a socialite
Adored, invited, pursued by publicists.
TOMORROW, I will be an outcast,
Have we met? I can't remember when.

YESTERDAY, I was a skeptic,
Believing, hoping, fearing nothing.
TODAY, I am a believer.
Concerning most things, a fanatic.
TOMORROW, I will be a skeptic,
Believing, hoping, fearing, nothing.

YESTERDAY, I was a coward,
Cringing at the very thought of wars.
TODAY, I am a soldier.
Counting notches on my sword.
TOMORROW, I will be a coward,
Hurting from my many scars.

YESTERDAY, I was a fool,
Having neither letters nor philosophies.
TODAY, I am wise, a learned gentleman,
With letters, graduate of the finest school.
TOMORROW, I will be a fool,
Forgetting where I left my trousers.

YESTERDAY, I was a sinner,
A disgrace to the human race.
TODAY, I am a Saint,
Who has found a loving Saviour.
TOMORROW, I will be a Saint,
For God will keep me by His Grace.

YESTERDAY, He was the Word,
The Architect of all creation.
TODAY, He is still the Living Word.
The Savior of every Nation.
TOMORROW, He's still the eternal Word,
Giver of life, Architect of our Salvation.

Prince John Chaber

PART III

PEOPLE I MET

THE CAT LOVER

One hot Summer's day when the sun steamed down with almost malignant vengeance and there was not the slightest hint of a breeze anywhere, I met a strange man on the highway.

He told me that he was driving his car along the fast lane, when he saw a passing motorist hit a young kitten and drove on without stopping. Needless to say, the young animal was killed instantly.

Big deal, I thought to myself. I have just walked along this very highway for the last five miles. True I was not struck and killed. But no one stopped for me.

While he was speaking to me, he was holding the dead animal tenderly, pressed closely to his chest and muttering over and over again. "The brute, the brute. People like that should be locked away."

I noticed, that his shirt and hands were saturated with the blood of the lifeless animal; but he did not seem to care.

My own feelings notwithstanding, I decided that this caring soul could turn out to be just the person I needed to help me out of my own predicament, so I muttered a few commiserating words of my own, and expressed the right sentiments about how the law should deal with reckless drivers on our roads.

I continued chatting a while with my new found friend, mostly listening to his complaints and sharing the burden of his grief, hoping that it would soon subside and we could both address what was really my main concern, namely, asking him for a lift.

I must confess that while I never particularly liked cats, in fact to be quite truthful I hated them for the very reason that most people love them, I would not deliberately run one over either. But if one got run over accidentally, I would not lose any amount of sleep over it.

I still remember the first time my mother brought home one of the little furry creatures. For that was what it looked like to me then. To my mind, it was just a large rodent and I hated rodents.

I was rocking on my grandmother's favorite rocking chair when it jumped into my lap and began curling up its back and purring sleepily. I was so incensed, that I threw it forcefully to the floor.

My mother, as it was her wont, gave me a severe spanking and I swore to myself that I would get even with this offensive creature. I did. A few days later it disappeared without a trace. However, I will spare the reader an account of the sordid details.

After that, there were two or three others, all of which disappeared likewise. My mother made extensive enquiries, but she never found out how, or why her pets were just vanishing.

One day, she came very close to accusing me of being in some way implicated. At her first hint, however, I protested my innocence most vehemently, and she backed off. But had she pressed, I am sure I would have blurted out my contempt for the despicable creatures, thereby giving myself away.

She informed me that it was seven years bad luck to kill a cat. I thought about that. But I decided that seven years, seven hundred years, back luck could not be as bad as the thrashing I would get if I confessed to disposing of her precious cats.

The upshot of it all, was that, she never brought any more cats to our home. She concluded that she was not "lucky" with cats. But I often wondered whether it was her maternal instincts, coupled with a desire to protect me from myself, that colored her decision to abandon the idea of keeping cats.

I cannot remember the exact details of the calculations I made way back then. But I do recall that, when I took into account the cats that vanished without a trace from our home, and all the others, stray and domesticated from around the village, I figured that, even if I lived to a ripe old age, plus or minus ten years, I would be dead for at least a hundred years before my good luck would return.

However, to each his own. I needed a ride and this cat-lover appeared to be my only hope. Accordingly, I was prepared to wait patiently on him until he was ready to fully recognize my presence. In the meantime I would make appropriate responses to his grief and hope that he would not spend too much more time over the dead animal.

Finally he rose, still holding the dead kitten tenderly to his breast.

He said. "I will take it home and bury it in my back yard."

At that moment I said to him. "Sir, I have walked along this highway for over 5 miles. My car broke down on the road back there and I have been trying to get to a phone to call for help. Would you be so kind as to give me a lift to the nearest gas station or a telephone?"

"No," he said, rather gruffly.

"Very well, Sir," I said. "But would you call this number for me when you reach a telephone? I will give you the money for the call," I ventured.

"Go away and leave me alone," the man said, as he abruptly turned away from me and gently laid the dead cat on the front seat, got into his car and drove off.

How strange, I thought to myself. So much love for a dead cat. So little concern for me. A human being. Well? I met such a man.

Perhaps it was one more leaf from the pages of misfortune written in the book of life. Perhaps, too, that ill-luck does follow those who ill attend cats. Or maybe it was a fitting nemesis, a natural sequence to, a dark chapter in the story of life of a little cruel and uncaring boy.

Not that I was cruel or uncaring towards animals generally. I loved dogs, especially if they were our own. If they belonged to other people and they were kept tied, at a distance, or under proper control, they were alright too.

In fact I often wondered why I loved dogs, as terrified as I sometimes were of them and hated cats which were docile and never did me any harm. I am sure I would have loved them too, if only they were not so presumptuous and purred and sniffed in the disgusting manner they do.

Dogs, on the other hand, possessed a daring and menace that appealed to me as a boy. And they were so intelligent too!

I remember this dog that I had to pass every afternoon. It would invariable bark at and run after me. It never came into the road. But it would often come so close that I could almost feel the blood flowing from the punctured wounds in my leg, and feel the warmth of its breath, as it snapped threateningly at me.

I would invariably arm myself with two stones and thus secure a sort of entente between the dog and myself. It never bit me and I never struck it.

This scene between the dog and myself must have been played-over a thousand times. Then one day, as I approached, I armed myself as usual with two stones. As I got opposite to the dog, I saw it lying in the yard.

It looked up at me and I tensed myself, expecting the same old routine. But a strange thing happened. The dog just looked at me and after a few seconds, clearly decided that I was no longer an interesting prospect for fun and games and ignoring me, turned its head away.

I was so surprised at the dog's reaction that I said. "Good afternoon, dog." It did not respond and that dog never barked at me again. Whatever took place that afternoon, resulted in a lasting peace treaty between us.

Be that as it may, the cat-lover was gone; and the other cars were racing by oblivious of me and my situation. I was left with no choice but to continue the gruesome trek along the highway.

After about another mile, I came to a little Inn; and gratefully I stopped to rest my weary body and tired feet and have a glass of ale.

And who should I find there but the very man, "the brute," to use the language of the cat-lover, who had killed the little kitten?

Well, brute or not, that turned out to be a lucky break for me. After listening to my story, he was all love, compassion and understanding. He offered to have my car towed to his own garage and promised to have it fixed free of costs. Then he drove me the 10 or so miles to my home.

"Why would you do all of this for me?" I asked.

"I don't really know," he replied "Perhaps it is your account of your meeting with that sanctimonious hypocrite."

"You see, I love animals, and although I do not care particularly for cats, I try not to kill anything on the road. But that little creature ran right across the highway in front of me. I had no choice. I knew once I hit it was dead instantly. I saw no point in stopping. But to be frank, I had no particular feelings of remorse either. People should not allow their pets to stray unto the highway."

"On the other hand, I do love and care for people. When you walked into that Inn, you looked dead beat. It was clear that you were having a hard time. I am no philanthropist, mind you. But if I can do something to brighten up the life of an individual, I do it."

"Perhaps it was my lucky day after all," I interjected. At least, it sure turned out that way. It was pure luck that I should have found you here."

But he interrupted me.

"Let us call it a happy coincidence," he said. "I do not particularly believe in luck, good or bad, although I never ridicule people who do."

"You said it was lucky that you met me here. But then, you would have to also say it was lucky that your car broke down. And even though you may be prepared to say so ex post facto, would you have said so if you had not met me and had to walk all the way home? But it was that very breakdown which triggered the series of meetings and events that followed. Your meeting with the sanctimonious hypocrite, posing as an animal lover. Your long trek along the highway. Your loss of faith in human nature. Your meeting with me; and the restoration of your faith. They are all part of the same series, and stem from a single common causation."

"But can the same incident be simultaneously lucky and unlucky? I venture not, unless it is conceded that luck is a purely subjective entity. But, it is my contention that if phenomena cannot be measured objectively, then any conclusions arrived at in the absence of objectivity, is to be mainly if not wholly discounted. For it is only when facts and circumstances are weighed in the scales of pure reason, can any accurate and meaningful conclusions be arrived at."

"Life, I believe is a series of pairs of opposites. Good and evil are two of them. Positive and negative are two others. Each day we encounter positive or negative influences in our lives in accordance with a complicated series of actions and reactions which impact us negatively or positively depending on a whole range of facts and circumstances forming part of a complex equation."

"The same facts and circumstances, the very same event affect different people in different and often opposite ways. We interpret these phenomena, objectively or subjectively and we reach conclusions which we call luck according to how we allow these conclusions to affect or impact our lives."

"For example, a passenger misses her flight, by only a few minutes. She is livid with rage. Her first reaction is to curse her stars, and anyone else whom she thinks might be responsible for, or contributed to, her missing her flight.

"What bad luck," she might say.

Then, within seconds, she sees the airplane that took off without her, explode in mid-flight before her very eyes and everyone on board is killed.

She goes into shock, and when she recovers, she becomes hysterical at the thought of herself being blown to bits; but as the days go by and the full force of her providential escape impinges more and more vividly on her consciousness, she says, "I thank my lucky stars." At least everyone tells her she should do so."

Preposterous is it not? Cursed be the stars in one breath. Thanks to the stars in another! You see how tenuous a thing luck is? Not a sufficiently sound base on which to rest so precious an entity as a human life. Wouldn't you say?

"Millions of persons take part in a lottery, each thinks he has the perfect reason for winning. But one wins and not the others. For the winner it is good luck. For the losers it is bad luck. But the winning numbers are the same. Were they lucky or unlucky?"

"On a particular night, there is a severe thunderstorm. Some people are glad, because, they have a perfect excuse for not turning out to work. Others are disappointed, because their property is damaged and they are not covered by insurance. But the people waiting to test a new radar system to see how it would react in a thunderstorm are ecstatic. For them, it is perfect weather."

"You see the point?" He asked "Nos te nos facimus fortuna deam!" "It is we who make thee, Fortune a Goddess."

He looked at his watch and smiled. "There I go again," he said.

"Well, you are quite a philosopher," I responded. "I am impressed."

I did not necessarily agree with all he said; but I had to admit that there was a great deal of logic, and therefore, weight, in his argument.

As he got into his car and drove away, I could not help saying out aloud, "what an interesting person, and I don't even remember his name, although he did tell it to me back there at the Inn."

True to his word, my car was delivered to my home the following day, all repaired and ready to go. I marveled at that man hard and uncaring towards a cat, but warm and loving toward a human being, even to a stranger he did not know.

That night, I dreamt of both men. I was walking on the surface of an endless sea, the waters of which had neither a ripple nor a wave.

The water was so crystal clear in fact that notwithstanding its great depth, I could see to the green, glossy, bottom which was teaming with every variety of fish imaginable.

There were fish of every size and shape and color and hue, all swimming together and basking in the calm serenity at the bottom of that great ocean. There were sharks, dolphins, porpoises, and great whales; and there were robins, mackerels, snappers and myriad small schools of fish. But there was no hostility among them. There was no fear, because, there was no danger.

As I stood there transfixed by the beauty and the serenity of the piscatorial paradise and enamored by the delights of its marine cosmopolitanism, I heard the humming of the sweet notes of a familiar hymn, and in a moment I as transported to the soft endless kaleidoscope of the sparkling sands along the shore.

There, sitting serenely on the shore by the side of the sea, was my benevolent philosopher and friend the cat-slayer.

He gave me a most knowing smile; but before I had time to wonder its meaning I heard a deafening and heart-rendering scream, coming as it were, from the very depth of the earth below my feet.

In another instant the sound appeared to be coming from just beyond a ridge overlooking the sea. I took off like a frightened bird and landed at the top of the hill in order to determine the source of that terrible scream.

No sooner had I landed on the hill than the earth began to tremble as if shaken by a gigantic earthquake.

As I looked toward the base of the hill, I saw a great chasm; and there, trapped hopelessly between two huge rocks was the cat-lover.

Without thinking, my first impulse was to jump in after him; and I might have done so , were it not for a restraining arm placed on my shoulder. I looked around to see my friend the cat-slayer smiling ever so benignly at me.

"No," he said. "No one who goes down into that place ever comes forth again. Besides the gulf between is and them is too great."

I watched helplessly as the cat-over disappeared into a caldron of boiling, foaming, lava. His scream as I saw him for the last time was as awesome as it was deafening.

I shuddered; and as I did so, I heard the cock crow thrice. And I knew I was not dreaming anymore. Yet, in my waking moments, I often reflect on those two men.

Each time I see a cat running frantically across the street, the all too vivid memory of the cat-lover would flash into my mind and the hopeless, pathetic, last look on his face, would haunt me like some irrepressible ghost for days on end.

I would often wonder if there is really such a place as that which appeared to be the final destination of the cat-lover. Some lines I had scribbled in my notebook many years before came flooding back into my memory.

If there is yet another hell,
Where the souls of men relent,
Then let the dead their anguish tell,
That all the living may repent.
For life is but a living hell,
So, should there be another?
Let us heed the warning well
And find a better place up yonder.
And if, indeed, there is a heaven,
It is clear what men should do.
Tread the path straight and even.
Shun that tormented place below.
To suffer once on earth should be,
But suffering full enough.
Still a second life in purgatory?
Oh, no, my friends, that's tough.

But then, too, I would think often of my friend the cat-slayer and wonder if he was right when he said that there was no such thing as luck.

I recalled when I was a bridge fiend, and I would play every night in the week if I got half a chance. There was a member of the group, one of the better players, who believed that luck was at least seventy five percent of the game.

Whether he won or lost, would often depend on whether he saw a black cat on his way to bridge. If he saw one at the side of the road, well it was going to be a rough night for him; but if it ran across him it was going to be a disaster. The odd thing was, it always turned out the way he said it would.

For myself, I will always remember the night, above all others, when the cards just loved me. I could do nothing wrong. I was able to open the bidding every hand, and to bid and make games and slams in abundance.

If partner opened the bid, I could make a positive response. If I needed a finesse, it worked. If I needed the trumps to be split in a certain way to bring the contract home, they were.

It was almost an embarrassment. At one stage, not being a completely selfish player, I found myself wishing that the cards would leave me alone for a while. After all, it is no fun for your opponents, just to know that they also played. Just passing and defending hand after hand with no hope of even the occasional set can be very devastating.

"Boy you are really hot tonight," my opponents kept lamenting, as I brought home slam after slam.

"I have never seen such luck," was one despairing comment as I brought home a slam doubled redoubled with three aces out against me.

But at that precise moment the telephone rang. It announced that my nemesis had arrived in town, and all hell was about to break loose.

Since that night, I have never had such luck. If I had I would never have played bridge again. It is an odd thing; but my bridge-player friend, who was so mortified by the sight of a cat, was fond of saying, "fortune favors the brave."

However, while not fawning to the whims of Lady Luck, or treating her as some Imperial Goddess, I have learnt not to turn a deaf ear or a blind eye, to her subliminal wooing or her subtle advances.

THE TWO CLERICS

Many years ago, I met two clerics who were engaged in a bitter argument. It happened that they shared the same rectory house at the time and it was the merest chance that I became a sort of unofficial mediator between them, a situation that I did not relish, to say the least.

One of the antagonists was white and the other black. But color was not the issue, save that, their differing ethnic backgrounds, might have contributed, to some extent, to their respective dispositions and divergent idiosyncrasies.

More to the point, however, is that one was an old man, and no doubt set in the ways of the good old days, and the other young, relatively speaking, and affected by the vicissitudes and upheavals of the sixties.

This I believe, was the single most important factor, and the root cause of their antagonism one toward the other, although, as all too often is the case, many erroneously concluded that it was a racial dispute.

It is one of those oddities of life, which is truly odd. Two white men have a dispute? It is a dispute. Two black men have a similar dispute? It is a riot. A white man and a black man have a dispute? It is a racial dispute.

The news media are particularly guilty, whether consciously or unconsciously of fanning the flames of racial hatred and division by the divisive and emotionally charged way they report the news.

A crime is committed. A white man is arrested. The news media report, if by radio, a man is arrested. The television media report, a man is arrested; and as a rule, no pictures.

If, however, the person arrested is a black man, the radio say, a black man was arrested. The television reporter says, a black man was arrested and without fail, pictures are provided.

Whatever attempts may be made to promote and propagate racial harmony in this world of ours, nothing of meaningful and durable significance will be achieved, until slurs, labels and taints, are effectively eradicated and put not on the back burner, but buried in the slime pits along with bigotry, ignorance, prejudice and hate.

However, the immediate cause of the dispute between the two clerics, was this. The younger cleric was walking home when it began to rain. The older man drove up in his car, stopped, looked in the face of the walking man and drove on when he realized who it was.

The younger man was naturally angry and demanded to know why he was so shabbily treated, particularly because, inter alia, the car belonged to the Parish, thus entitling him to its equal use.

"I would have sooner stopped for a dog," was the old vicar's caustic reply.

Well, that was the cue for those two men of God literally to fly at each other's throat. They both gnashed and snarled like angry dogs and said some really nasty and mean things to each other.

At that point, they were both out of control, and frankly, so was I. I shouted at the top of my voice for calm. But it took a lot of shouting and several minutes before either took the slightest notice of me.

When at last I was able to make myself heard, after a slight lull in the storm, I said "gentlemen, gentlemen, wait a minute, I am witnessing this; but I cannot believe it is really happening. "Where is the love? Where is the forgiveness, the understanding, the example?" But each was so busy decrying the lack of Christian virtue in the other, that they did not hear a word I said.

Finally when it was clear that nothing could be achieved by my continued presence, and utterly disgusted at what I just saw and heard and ruing the moment that I decided to set foot in that house, I left the scene as abruptly as I had come. As I went through the door they were still snarling at each other.

On my way home, I decided to buy my do a bone. When I arrived home, I fed my dog the precious morsel which he took with a relish, a sparkle in his eye and the wag of this tail.

No sooner had he lain down to his little feast than the neighbor's cat sauntered over and lay down beside him. To my surprise my dog, a full blooded hot tempered German Shepherd proffered to the neighbors cat one end of his bone, while he continued chewing on the other.

As I watched the two animals, who were supposed to be proverbial enemies of long standing lying, peacefully nibbling away in unison on their shared delicacy, and defying every archaic notion about the animosities of cats and dogs, I could not help wondering why two Parish Priests, both belonging to the same church, both simultaneously serving the same congregation, not to mention the same God, could not at least live as harmoniously as this dog and that cat. Yet I knew two such clerics.

THE VILLAGE PREACHER

In my village as a boy, I knew a man who was a Preacher in the local Adventist Church. One day I met him at the little village shop where he had just purchased a pound of sugar. The sugar was poured from the scales into his open cup; for that was the way sugar was often bought and sold, in that village in those days.

No sooner had he received his purchase than a fly, all too anxious to dive into the precious substance, dove headlong in and got stuck.

Much to my amazement the local Preacher caught the fly deftly and delicately between his fingers, and rather ostentatiously, held it up and then let it go.

In retrospect, I do confess that it was somewhat presumptions of me' but I said to the Preacher. "You pious, self-righteous, fool. Don't you know that flies spread germs and that within forty eight hours there will be thousands more like that laying their filthy eggs all over the place and infection everything they touch?"

Now, I will not argue that, particularly as a boy of thirteen or fourteen, or fifteen or sixteen, I was right to call this grown man a fool, or to speak to him in so disrespectful a manner. If he had slapped me across the ears with an open hand, I would have thoroughly deserved it. But in my defense I was young and impressionable. Precocious, perhaps, but not rude.

It should be appreciated, too, that I really detested flies, and my chagrin was more directed at the thought of sparing a filthy, germ infested fly, than against the Preacher as such.

Be that as it may, however, my remarks so outraged the Preacher that he raised his walking stick to strike me on the head and would have doubtless floored me, if I did not have good presence of mind. I sang out for all the world to hear and see. "You see this hypocrite here, he cannot kill a fly' but he has raised his cane to floor me, a mere boy."

Needless to say, the logic of my words cut him to the quick' and there he was, his stick raised, ominously, threateningly' but frozen in mid air. His eyes burning with hatred, or was it just plain anger? I truthfully do not know. He did not strike me but he never spoke to me again after that.

In my village, at that time, it was regarded as particularly rude and ill-mannered and still is up to this day, to pass anyone on the street at any time of the day or night without an appropriate word of greeting.

However, after that incident with the fly, the Preacher never responded to my greetings. But here again, maybe he never heard me.

One thing I do know with absolute certainty and it is this. I have also met other men like the Preacher. I often refer to them as "blood thirsty pacifists." I usually do my best to avoid such men. If I need have anything to with them, I try to do it and get it over with as quickly as possible and move on.

Conscientious objectors, are often also such men. They are, make no mistake about it, a very dangerous and odious breed of men; but I have met such men also.

Unfortunately, there are plenty of them in the world. They will beat you to death in the name of peace.

Another species but of the same genus, are many so called champions of freedom, liberty and justice.

I once met a man who described himself as a Freedom Fighter. In what was supposed to be an address to whip up international support for his group and their cause, he harangued his audience mercilessly for nearly two hours with a myriad of fancy, high-sounding phrases, such as Liberty, Equality, Justice, Freedom, Human Rights, Democracy, The Rule of Law.

At long last, he was finished and I was able to get a question in. "Tell me, Sir," I asked. "Tell me, as briefly as possible who are you primarily fighting against?"

"Our white oppressors," he said with rapier like sharpness.

"Well then," I followed up, "If you are fighting for freedom and all the other noble causes you mentioned, would you care to comment on the reports about the hundreds of your own people whom you slay on a daily basis?

"That's a good question," he said with a rather impish smile. "you see, we don't shoot people. We shoot ideas. But where do people carry ideas? In their heads. So that to get at the ideas, we have to shoot at the head. Well? Sometimes people do get killed and quite often people other than the actual enemy."

"But, you may ask who is the enemy. As I have said before, our main enemy in Africa is the white man. But often the black man gives comfort and support to the white man, and aids and abets him in his war against us."

Not only does he work for the white man, and join his forces against us, his black brothers, he allows the white man to brainwash him and use him as a vehicle for the dissemination of his ideology and racist propaganda. In that case, even our black brother is no longer a brother, but an enemy. Everyone knows the white man's strategy toward the black man. Divide and rule."

"Do you realize what the face of Africa would look like if it was united, under one rule, one government, with the divisive and inimical influence of the white man finally eliminated? My friends, the white man trembles at the thought of such a day."

"Not only do they see a unified continent as a threat to their sources of raw materials, the main source from which they have been able to amass wealth and riches, and build empires over the centuries, at the expense of the African Nations' a unified Africa would mean the consolidation of the largest single ethnic group in the world into one camp, thereby, giving poignancy to the really practical and de facto divisions of the world, and putting the racial balance into proper perspective."

"You see, my friend, all the artificial barriers, cunningly erected by the machinations of the imperialist minds, have to come down. Only then will the true divisions be clearly seen."

"The world is not divided East/West, North/South, Rich/Poor, Haves/Have-nots. It is not Democracy versus Communism. Those barriers, in so far as they exist, are purely artificial and incidental. The only true barrier, the only real division, is between black and white."

"Take the great United States. Do you think that with all its mighty power, and all its capacity for international double dealing, destabilization and intrigue, not to mention its military clout, the odious South African regime would have been able to stand if it were not for the overt and covert support of the United States and the other major powers?"

"For almost three decades, we have heard talk about the cold war, in general, and the great Communist, threat, in particular. We in Africa and the rest of the Third World, as we have been stigmatized, are supposed to join in the fight against the spread of Communism. But let the Communist Empire break up tomorrow, as indeed I am convinced it eventually will. And let reports reach the West to the effect that the a group of White Russians are being slaughtered by a set of White Russians. Then we will see how quickly the Americans and the rest of the white world move to intervene and stop the killings."

"But do they care if white South Africans butcher 10,000 black Africans every hour? Of course not. Whatever they may say, whatever pretentious shows they put on, whatever the hypocritical masks they wear, it is an inescapable and irrefutable fact. White people do not like black people and that is that. No ifs, ands, or buts about it. The only difference, as we move from white country to white country, and from white community to white community, is the degree of expression of that which lies within and motivates the white man's hatred of the black man."

"On the other hand look at the way America treats its non white citizens. First off, the Indians were killed off and those who escaped the slaughter, were incarcerated on the reservations."

"Then came the advent of the blacks. Even after two hundred years of living and working, or fighting in the first war of independence, a massive domestic war and two conflicts, fighting and dying for their country, blacks are still treated as third class citizens."

"At the same time, any white man from any part of the world, including the very countries whose aggression the black man has given his life to repulse, Germany, Japan, The Soviet Union, can enter and settle in the United States without let or hindrance and almost immediately, he is a first class citizen."

"I have no illusions, either that The Soviet Union is even less favorably disposed toward the black man. Should there be any doubt about this point, a good indicator would be to look at the way they have treated their own serfs and minorities over the years."

"A school friend of mine went to Moscow, a few ears ago, to study political science. The Russian authorities, eager to indoctrinate him into the Soviet way of life, endeavored to make an apt student and disciple out of him. He was allowed to meet and hobnob with people in the highest circles. He was a frequently invited to parties and on social occasions. Their libraries, museums and other facilities of education and learning were all at his disposal; but they left him no doubt that Russian girls were definitely off limits to him."

"The Professors and Tutors went out of their way, though, to make sure he had a thorough, Soviet education. Most especially, they were at pains to point out the various attributes of the communist system over democracy, not least among the defects of which was the terrible racial barriers installed by the Imperialist hypocrites, America and Britain."

"Your people, Obe, were brought to America from Africa in chains over two hundred years ago. Today they are still in shackles. Only for economic reasons the chains were placed around their ankles, confining them to the fields and barns like common beasts of burden, with little food, inadequate shelter and bereft of dignity."

"Today, the chains are removed from the ankles, but placed about their necks, for economic reasons, choking them, like animals trapped in a cage, being fed with crumbs, sleeping in shelters, and dying if they but seek to establish but their common dignity. So you see, my friend Obe, it is true that things have changed for the black man in America' but they have only changed for the worse."

"At last, my friend was deemed to have made good progress after attending the Moscow University for just over a year. It was time to put what he had learnt to the test."

"Well, my dear Obe, his professor asked him. What would you say is the basic difference between freedom of speech in Russia and freedom of speech as it exists in the West?"

Without hesitation, my friend replied. "In the West, you remain free after the speech." He was promptly deported."

If the Freedom Fighter's intention was to raise a laugh, he succeeded. While I perceived a good deal of truth and could identify with much of what was contained in his long rambling reply to my question, I felt that his answer was in part designed to add humor to what was a serious question, thereby down-playing his rather cavalier reference to shooting ideas out of the head.

Primarily for that reason, I did not think his answer was at all funny. Since, however, there was a room full of people who had their hands up, and who had, perhaps less provocative questions of their own, I perceived that further dialogue with the Freedom Fighter would not have been appropriate in the circumstances. But, oh, how I wished I could have take a shot or two at some of his own ideas, since I am no pacifist. But then, I am no freedom fighter either.

It did occur to me, however, that those who were slain for their ideas, in someone else's pursuit of liberty, now had neither life nor liberty' and still there is no end in sight to the conflict in South Africa in particular and Africa in general. It would seem that the insemination of ideals by the assassination of ideas does not work. But such is one of the cruel ways of life.

If indeed the word is mightier that the sword, it would seem to me that a mighty number of innocent souls have perished in vain in that bloody land called Africa. A land where the cries of the slain can be heard above the daily cut and thrust and constant clanging of the cruel sword of brute beasts, whose thirst for blood knows no parallel and whose wicked hearts know no bounds. A land lost in a world conveniently blind to the rivers of blood flowing there, and deliberately deaf to the cries of a people, helpless to ward off the barbarity of the genocidal war being waged against them, are counted less than sheep for the slaughter.

THE CHRISTIAN

When I was a teenager, I knew a man who called himself a Christian. As far as I am aware, I never did or said anything to cause him the slightest offence. However, to be fair, I was rather sweet on his step-daughter, who was around my age, fourteen or fifteen' but there was nothing in that affair to justify, even remotely, my being marked for death.

One day, as I was traversing a lonely mountain pass, I met that Christian man travelling in the opposite direction on his donkey.

The roadway was narrow rocky and uneven, being severely washed and eroded by constant heavy rains, and the constant ebb and flow of hoofed and unhoofed traffic.

Consequently, as we were passing alongside each other, he was elevated somewhat above me, on a high embankment on one side of the road, while I had to pass below him on the other.

At the moment he was precisely adjacent to and over me, he raised his cutlass to split my skull open, intending I am sure to murder me there and then. I saw the raised weapon, held menacingly and in a flash, I caught the mean and murderous look in the eye of my assailant. The fact that he only had one eye, seemed to accentuate even more the malignity in his one good, or should I say, evil eye.

It all happened so suddenly and so unexpectedly, I had not time to think or react in any way. I was terrified. I do not now recall what if any thoughts I had in those fleeting moments. But I do remember thinking, "Oh God, this is it."

Whatever I might or might not have said then, however I might or might not have reacted, one thing I do say now, and it is this. No man dies, before the hour of his death. Here was an assailant poised to murder me. His weapon already sent on its cruel way. There was I entirely at his mercy and the inscrutable face of fate.

Mercifully, at the very instant that his machete was in a downward arc, his donkey faltered and veered away from me and in a few more ambles he was gone' and being young and fleet of foot, I, too, was away as swiftly as a mountain goat.

"How could such an evil man call himself a Christian?" I asked myself, when about a half an hour later, my heart slowed down sufficiently to allow my thoughts to function. What have I ever done to this man? We were practically neighbors, my parent and himself were on good terms as far as I knew, and I never told him, "look his eye black," to us a local expression. Why then did he try to murder me?

The thing worried me for a long time. But I kept the details of his attempt on my life and my providential escape to myself. As things turned out, it was three or four days before I saw him again.

Since his attack on me, I used to dread such a meeting. How would I react? How would he react? I used to ask myself. It was in one of the local grocery shops. As I approached it, I could hear his voice and his coarse laughter inside.

Somehow, I found the courage to walk boldly in. As I entered, his good eye seemed to see me many moments before his feeble brain was able fully to grasp the fact of my sudden appearance. Even so, on seeing me, the light in that eye appeared to fade like an oil lamp that was slowly running out of fuel.

When at last my presence fully impinged upon his consciousness, he choked. The words that were on his lips were cut off and surprised, everyone looked around as I entered sensing the sudden change in his demeanor. Our three eyes met for a moment. I had a slight advantage, I thought because I was on his dark side. I wondered what blinded his other eye. Wish to God you had lost both eyes I swore beneath my breath.

Some one must have seen the malevolence in my countenance, or sensed the tenseness in the atmosphere. So he said, "is something wrong?"

At the question, the Christian froze. I saw the discomfiture in his face and by this time, the light was entirely out of his eye. At that moment he was Polyphemus groping for his sheep.

I allowed the question to hang for a while. This would-be murderer was groveling, groping and uncomfortable and I was enjoying watching him, in a spiteful and contemptuous sort of way.

The chatter and the laughter had died and it seemed that the Christian was about to do so also. I could see the thought grinding over slowly in his feeble brain. "Was he going to accuse me now? Was he going to tell these people that I tried to kill him? Perhaps he has informed the police and he is here waiting for them to arrive."

Then he froze. At first I thought he had died. Or was it that I merely wished it? Then I saw that he was still breathing, and beads of sweat were forming on his face. His jaw dropped and he slumped over on the counter on which he was leaning before. His face was rough and unshaven and the irregular growth of curled up grey and black hair made him appear even more grotesquely disgusting.

I was savoring the satisfaction of the moment. Oh, how sweet a thing is revenge, I thought. And how true is the saying that, "the guilty conscience needs no accuser." Then I noticed the eyes of everyone staring at some object behind me. I turned and looked, and there blocking the doorway, was the broad, familiar frame of the police sergeant from the nearby police station.

As usual, his khaki uniform was stained with sweat and I got the distinct sensation of horse manure, as I always did when I was close to that officer. I often wondered whether the odor was that of himself or the horse he always rode, when he came to the village on police duty.

"Everyone behaving themselves?" asked the officer.

There were the usual shifting and grumbles of assent in response to the officer's question; but for my part I said nothing.

"And how about you, young man?, he asked turning directly to face me.

I stood and stared deliberately at the officer and then shifted my gaze to look intently at my would-be killer, as though I was tongue tied or too timid or too scared to speak.

Of course I was playacting. I was not called the drama king of my school for nothing. I wanted the Christian to grovel. I wanted him to sweat and sweating he was profusely.

I was now the center of attention. Everyone was looking at me to hear what I would say since I was known to be never at a loss for words. Everyone present knew me and knew me well.

On the other hand I did not particularly care for this officer. He was supposed to be a friend of my father's; but it was he who, sat at our dinner table one fine Sunday afternoon, wined and dined and then sent a gang of marauding police officers to search our home for contraband brandy.

I have never forgotten the incident. I remember his fat, bulky frame, sitting there at our dinner table and remarking in his peculiar singing accent, "My friend that was a very fine meal, very fine meal and this is very fine brandy."

Oh the number of time after that I wished he had choked if not on the meal, then on the brandy or both.

All these thoughts went through my head as I looked at the Christian and wished he would just die right there and then, strangled to death by his

84

guilty conscience, and the smelly over weight sergeant and wished that he and his horse would just fall over a cliff on their way back to the station.

I still did not answer the sergeant's question, as deliberately and intently I turned and walked through the door. While I was still within ear shot, the chatter and the laughter resumed and no doubt the drinking and the joviality.

Choke on your next drink, you bastards, I said to myself; but another little voice said to me.

"Silence, my child. For vengeance is mine."

That little voice stilled my anger somewhat, and where there was a hard lump of resentment if not actual hatred, it gradually gave way to a softer gentler feeling of sympathy, although not quite forgiveness. Sympathy for a man who would hold Christ in one hand and wield a murderous weapon in the other.

Finally I came to the conclusion that perhaps my would-be-murderer was a Christian after all, so that it was the very presence of Christ in his life that stayed his hand, or more accurately caused his donkey to falter and kept him from shedding my innocent blood and thereby becoming a murderer. Oh yes, I knew such a man.

Some time later, I heard a story about the Christian, how he had murdered his first wife and made it look like a cattle had gored her to death. I don't know if there was any truth in the allegations or how he was able to convince the authorities that his wife's death was an accident. But for my part I surely had proof positive that the man was capable of murder.

"Good Lord," I told myself after hearing the story, "I was really lucky that day!"

It was a long time after that I learnt that no man in this life can pass the boundary of his life which has been fixed and that conversely no man dies before he crosses that boundary.

I learnt, too, that the Master takes care of, defends and protects His own. That what attended me that day was blessing, not luck. For the Lord will cover the head of the defenseless under the shadow of His wings.

As I thought on these things, I remembered a story my father had told me about a soldier who was charged with failing to shoot an enemy soldier who was guarding the entrance to the enemy's compound.

In defense the soldier explained that as he approached the sentinel, he was singing a familiar hymn, "Jesus Lover of my Soul." All right, thought the soldier, it can't do any harm to let the man sing his hymn before killing him. But when the soldier heard the words of the hymn, "Cover my defenseless head, with the shadow of Thy wing," he just could not shoot.

Whatever others may think or feel or believe, I do believe that my defenseless head was covered not only by but under the wings of the Almighty that day and hence I live to tell the story.

MY FRIEND

There was a man whom I treated as a friend for years. I fed him with the milk of kindness and invited him to drink from the very depth of my little fountain of knowledge. He was an avaricious recipient and I was a cheerful giver.

I did notice, however, that my friend never tried to give me anything in return, although he often boasted about the rapid growth of his worldly storehouse of wealth. But that fact never affected my continued giving or my attitude toward him in the least. For my soul taught me early that giving, true Christian giving, comes from a cheerful heart; and a cheerful heart lacks nothing.

But, alas, that friend opened up his mouth and set forth his heart to wound me mortally for no other reason than sheer wickedness.

In a way, I was partly to blame. I had been warned repeatedly by friends and foes alike, that I had befriended a man whose only friend was himself. Time and time again, I obtained cogent first hand evidence of his treachery. But yet, while never taking my eyes off him completely, I did continue to treat and regard him as a friend.

I took no heed of the repeated warnings, and I ignored both the jarring of my own senses and the clear evidence, gathered in many ways, of the man's total unreliability and untrustworthiness.

Eventually, I paid a very large price for my magnanimity, though some would call it stupidity. It is aptly said that, "a reconciled friend is a double enemy." If that is so, it would follow that a re-re-reconciled friend, is deadly. I do not know that I have learnt any particular lesson from the calamity that my friend caused me. But I will venture this much. If you keep a rattlesnake as a companion, it behoves you not ever to take your eyes off it. And never, never, turn your back on it.

One evening I was lying on my bed in deep introspection, and ruminating over the seriousness of the wounds inflicted on me by my friend, when my thoughts drifted back in time to the memory of a dog I once had.

She was a beautiful dog, intelligent, alert, protective. But I was having trouble training it to open and close a particular door that would facilitate her calls in the night.

After trying all the usual methods of house breaking her, she would still have occasional lapses and so, on a particular morning, I lost my patience, and in a fit of anger, I gave my dog a severe thrashing, not with a rolled-up newspaper, as I hitherto used as a training tool, but with my leather strap.

It was then that I learnt the true meaning of the phrase "as shamed as a dog." For hours after the beating, my dog could not look at me, averted my eyes and refused to eat. She had no illusions with regard to what she had done wrong. I remembered that as soon as I stopped beating it, it came and licked my hand. It never had anymore lapses after that.

I was reflecting on my dog, and how heart broken I was when she was taken out for a walk by my maid and allowed to be run over by a reckless driver, when I fell asleep.

While I slept, I had a most revealing dream. In my dream I stood at heaven's gate. As I waited, there was a long line of eager souls, also waiting to get into heaven. And lo and behold, who should materialize beside me but my very friend and my good old dog!

While we thus waited in that ethereal presence, my erstwhile friend was in an instant transformed into the very image of my dog and my dog changed into my friend.

Just then, an angel appeared, in saintly attire and with unceremonious solemnity announced.

"No dogs allowed."

At the very next moment my transformed friend and I were ushered into the Pearly Gates and as they were shut behind us the dog was whisked away, kicking and screaming, whining, and protesting. The last time I saw it, it was being swallowed up by a very dark and ominous looking cloud.

What a pity, I thought to myself. I saw in my minds eye the reincarnation of the good and pious man of Islington, and the mad dog of whom Goldsmith wrote, in his "Elegy on the Death of a Mad Dog."

"At first, that dog and man were friends;
But when a pique began,
The dog, to gain some private end,
Went mad and bit the man.
The wound it seemed both sore and sad,
To every Christian eye;
And while they swore the dog was mad,
They swore the man would die.
But soon, a wonder came to light,
That how the rogues, they lied.
The man recovered of the bite,
The dog it was that died."

And what is the moral of this story? That even good dogs do not go to heaven. No positively not.

VOICES

Part I
THE MUSICIAN

I knew a musician who took ill and went to the local hospital. After he had been there for sometime, the doctors announced that nothing was wrong with him.

The hospital authorities told him he should go home and carry on with his life; but he refused. They ordered him to leave the hospital to make room for someone else who really needed medical attention; but he clung tenaciously to his bed. Eventually, he refused to get up; he refused to eat; he was, in his words, waiting for death.

It is said, "so a man thinks, so he is." How very, very true! There are many reported instances of persons, who, overtaken by some crippling injury or disease, just simply refuse to open the door to the destroyer death, however urgently, or demandingly, or menacingly, he knocks. The reports of such tenacity in the face of the great and terrible reaper are many.

There are numerous reports of instances where, even the awful executioner was forced to back away in the face of such great defiance. But conversely, there are also volumes of cases where people just simply die, because they, from one cause or another, have lost the will to live.

The musician was such a person. He was a young man in his middle thirties; he was physically in good shape; but mentally he was a wreck. Convinced that he had been bewitched, he simply refused to resist and gave up. The ultimate result was in a sense, inevitable.

The case of the musician is of course, in stark contrast to that of the patient, who, a century earlier, when the horse was the commonest and swiftest form of transportation, caused something of a commotion at the same hospital in the middle of the night.

"Doctor, doctor," he shouted, as if in a demented state, "please lend me your fastest horse. I must leave this place at once."

"Why?" asked the sleepy-eyed doctor. "It is the middle of the night; and you are a very sick man. Where do you think you are going this late in the night and in your condition?"

"But doctor, you don't understand!" the patient explained, in his great agitation. "I have just seen death."

Well, so pathetic was his plea and so clearly alarmed was he, that the doctor gave him his swiftest horse, so that he may make good his escape.

"But where would you go? Asked the doctor, of the panic stricken man?

"Home to Rendezvous," was the man's short reply as he sent the horse flying away out of the coble-stoned hospital yard, guided only by a crescent moon.

A few minutes later, the doctor was returning to his office, and as he walked along one of the ill lit corridors, of the hospital, he met death.

"Death," said the doctor, "why did you frighten my patient so?"

"I did not frighten him," death replied, "I merely whispered to him that I was waiting for him at home."

One day, I visited the Musician in the hospital and as I was alone with him for sometime, I took the opportunity of looking at his chart going back over a period of several days.

It revealed that there was absolutely no clinical reason for his illness. There was nothing wrong with this man. Nothing physically, that is. But indeed this man was very, very sick in his mind, which is the worst part of the body to be affected. He was convinced that he was condemned to die and that nothing could reverse his fate.

I spoke to him for several minutes. I used every persuasive argument at my disposal. I appealed to his reason; but that had been on long leave. I tried to appeal to his survival instincts; but those had already deserted him. I searched in vain in the storehouse of his past for a rational argument which I could project as a reason for living; but without a logos, there was no available therapy.

That storehouse, which had served as the repository of all that one holds precious to life had been long stripped, and now lay hopeless and forlorn.

I attempted to project live images into the future, even to places near and far and bid him take a little walk with me, one step at a time one day at a time. But he said he was too weak to stand much less take a step. I offered to carry him. But he objected that he would be too heavy a burden, and bid me leave him to die in peace.

The nurse came in and announced that it was time for me to leave. In a final effort I said, "hang in there. I will be back to see you next week." But, alas, in less than a week and, before I could see him again, he passed on to the other side from which there is no return.

The news of the death of the musician saddened me greatly. Somehow, I felt there aught to be more I could have done. Perhaps the least I could have done was to stay away from the man in the first place. Still he was gone and there was nothing I could do about that, I told myself.

Then, out of nowhere, nowhere, that is, that I knew or recognized at the time, a voice, calm, yet agitated, friendly, yet hostile, controlled yet outraged, snapped back at me, with the words. "Oh yes there was!"

To say that I was startled would be an understatement. I was terrified. "What was that?" I asked out aloud. But there was no reply. " Oh well, it was my imagination,' I told myself. But was it? It certainly was not my voice and there was no one else in the room.

For several days thereafter, I kept listening for the voice to speak to me again, but there was nothing. Yet, I examined the words in my mind over and over again, searching for some clue as to their meaning. But I could find none.

"Alright," I said, "let me assume that I was not imagining things. What is it I could have done, or ought to have done but failed or omitted to do? After all I am not a doctor and I certainly do not believe in witchcraft. What then?" I could think of absolutely nothing.

The only think that made the slightest sense, or rather, nonsense was my use of the phrase, "hang in there." What an empty, totally useless and nonsensical phrase.

There was this dying man, literally without a leg to stand on; without the strength to stand even with the aid of a crutch. I gave him no crutch; I gave him no hope; but I ask him to hang on. But hang on to what, and for what purpose? I vowed never to use that phrase again in any circumstances.

Still, I never heard the voice again; and slowly, as the days ran into weeks and the weeks ran into months it began to recede into that area of the psyche where all the things we ascribe to imagination or fantasy have their abode. By and by the voice was scarcely a memory.

Part II
THE TORMENTED GIRL

Years later, I met a girl whose sad eyes told of unspeakable grief and the pain of living too many nights of fear. Her sadness troubled my spirit, and as she opened up her soul to me, I was quickly making her pain my pain and her suffering my suffering. Before I knew it, I was probing, searching the dark shadows beyond those melancholy eyes beyond which all her dark and painful secrets lay hidden.

Little by little, the dismal details of her dark experiences at the hands of her own father, was being unraveled; and, as she unveiled her dark secrets layer by layer, the sub strata of the hard core of fear was laid bare before my consciousness.

In the beginning, the fear of being sexually abused by her own father; and having to suffer in silence, coupled with the ever present treat of being killed should she expose him. After all, he was a man of the cloth!

Then, in more recent times, having fled from the scene of her ordeal, to a place where every gory detail of her torment was lived and relived in every sleeping moment she now lived under the conviction that he had bewitched her in retaliation for her running away from him.

It had taken several weeks, meeting once or twice a week, for the heavy shades drawn shut over her window of secrecy to be lifted. But once they were lifted, and light began to filter through, the darkness recedes and with it the weight of fear. For fear is nothing more than the weight of unlighted images trapped in a dark and dismal house of darkness. Once the windows of that house are opened up and its dark recesses and unaired crevices are exposed to the light and the fresh air, that weight, like stagnant air, is slowly dispersed.

However, at the mere mention of the word bewitched, my heart skipped a beat and my spirit recoiled. I was reminded all too vividly of my encounter with the Musician and how hopelessly I had failed him. This time I was not going to meddle. It was one thing dealing with nightmares, fear, buried secrets and all that kind of stuff; but not that other thing. The unconscious mind, dream theory, coping with fear; those were maters I did not mind messing about with. But the darker, murkier side of life, were areas I much preferred to steer clear of, particularly since my encounter with the Musician.

I must stop seeing this girl, I thought to my self. Somehow I must find a way of doing so, without causing her too much pain, or causing her to slump back into the gripping terrors of the past.

Suddenly, conveniently, I remembered that the time for a long earned vacation had arrived; and relieved at the prospects of a convenient way out, I started to explained to her that I was going to be away for the next several weeks and expressed the wish that she would be alright from there on.

But I must have sounded very unconvincing. For she said,

"Thanks, John, at least it was nice been able to talk to someone, especially someone as patient and understanding as you. These past weeks were a great relief for me. It's as though since I have been talking to you a great burden has been lifted off my shoulders. I feel so much better of late. I still have those awful nightmares; but they are not as frequent. And when they do recur they are not as frightening because often you would be there somewhere."

"At first, it was as if I was standing in a large circle and you were always right there on the edge, a vague shadow; but gradually you began to get closer and closer to the center of the circle. And then, no longer a mere shadow, but you, there in the flesh. All I had to do was say your name and you would be right there beside me."

"Sometimes, in my dream, I would find myself in the middle of a vast ocean, with a whole sea of sharks all around me; often one of the sharks, usually a great white, with sharp jet black teeth, would break away from the rest and start closing in on my fast.

Then I would scream out your name and I would wake up."

I was overwhelmed. Some words from the bible flooded into my memory. What were they? "He that put his hands to the plough and pull back is not worthy of his hire? I felt the tug of conscience and a feeling of guilt was beginning to settle over me. "You are about to turn your back on this girl after building her hopes up. She trusts you. She is relying on you to help her over whatever are the hurdles that she has to face.

"You were willing to walk with her in the valley. But now she has reached the foot of the hill, now she is at the most difficult part of her journey, you are running out on her."

"Well, I reasoned, being a coward is one think; but knowing when you are licked is quite another. The words from the bible, are not really relevant to the present situation. I am a volunteer, not a hireling. Just a Samaritan, using good old horse sense, to help this girl come to grips with her burden of fear. I am neither an old school Sigmund Freud, modern day Logo Therapist, nor a Head Shrink. I went in over my head once and what was the result? The truth is, I have done all I can. I have gone as far as I can go; and that is it."

I was neither satisfied nor convinced by my own reasoning. I was afraid that if I continued I would talk myself out of my decision and back into further trouble. So I said quickly. "Perhaps you should go and see a psychiatrist," but she shook her head.

"I don't want to do that, she said.

"Why not?" I asked, but I could see that her mind was made up.

"I don't know," she replied, "I only know I don't want to, and I can't."

It was clear that arguing with her would have been useless, and so, I said good-bye to her, promising to see her when I return from my vacation.

As I turned to leave, I could not help noticing a sadness in her eyes that I had never seen before. "Oh God" I muttered to myself. "What have I done?"

The following day I duly left for my vacation.. but every waking moment, my mind was returning to this girl and her problem. In addition, the look in her eyes was troubling he in a strange way.

I was not enjoying myself at all. I had attempted to run away from this girl and her problems. Even more to the point, I was worried and afraid over the strange, almost wistful look I had seen in her eyes.

Was I into this thing deeper than I anticipated, much, much, deeper than I even now know? Surely I had done or said nothing to precipitate this other crisis. "Hell," I said to myself. "Can a fellow not even do a decent thing in his life without, …without? Oh, heck, "I muttered to myself as I walked away.

My mind flashed back to something that I had read somewhere, sometime before. What was it? Ah yes. The imposter, Rutherford, I believe his name was, who went into this young girl's home, ostensibly to convert her to be a Jehovah Witness, but raped her and became an infidel. "But surely I had done nothing, consciously or unconsciously, that could be remotely interpreted as being improper. In all my dealings with this girl, I was on the up and up at all times, to use a colloquialism."

I have done my best, I reasoned and surely, no man can do better than his best. Was there anything I could have done differently. Not at all, I told myself. I have extended the balm of human compassion and kindness to this girl and there is nothing further I could have done

Yet there was the lingering feeling of dissatisfaction with myself. I felt that somehow in some way I had not done enough. I kept going back to the word bewitched. I told myself that had we not reached that hurdle, I would have continued working with her at least until the bad dreams had gone away. I did not believe that it was possible for anyone to bewitch another in a physical sense. But I was convinced that it was possible to inflict a persons mind so critically that hopelessness and even death may result.

Take the case of the witch doctor. His medicine, his most potent medicine, exists, in so far as it exists at all, only in the mind of members of his tribe or clan, who believe in his power. Without that implanted belief, his power is useless. It is the power of suggestion embedded in the mind, and activated under the halo of enchantments and hocus pocus, which is the effective tool that the witch doctor uses to first paralyze the will and then inflict the body.

It had that effect on the Musician, and only thus will it work. So why did I run away? The simple answer is I do not know. In retrospect, I felt, somewhat ashamed of myself for another reason.

Up to that time I had counseled many families who were having domestic problems, particularly with regard to their teenage daughters. I was particularly critical of parents who, on discovering that their teenage daughters were pregnant, threw, them out of their homes.

"Look, I would say, I do not know whose fault it is that your daughter is pregnant. The laying of blame is not the issue here. One thing I do know and it is this. The fault such as it is, must be born by both sides; but in what proportion I do not know and I really do not care. What I do care about is the fact that you have chosen the worst time in your child's life to abandon her."

"Let me ask you this, I would say. If she was married and living with her husband in a nice new house, you would rush to her side with all the love, devotion, caring and concern you could muster, would you not? Yet, here is your daughter, your own flesh and blood, pregnant, alone, having neither husband, house, or any of the comforts or amenities of life; particularly those things that a pregnant woman needs. And at this time you would abandon her?"

"Consider this also. If you send her out there, into the world; alone, forlorn and hopelessly lost, what good can she make of the rest of her life? I tell you truly, many convicted murderers would much prefer instant execution than a sentence of life imprisonment, if that sentence means having to spend the rest of their lives in incarceration, with only the memory of their crime for company. But, alas, what you are doing here is to sentence your daughter to a life sentence. To be confined in a prison of hopelessness and despair. A sentence from which there is likely to be no reprieve.

Then, in a different tone and as a final clincher, I would add. What you are in fact doing, is not so much throwing your daughter out, as in reality putting your problem away from you. You cannot face it. So you think by throwing it out of your house, as you would a discarded piece of furniture, you would not have to wake up and see it any more.

For whether you like it or not, pregnant or not, your daughter is your problem. You do not solve your problems by locking them away, no more than you can pay your debts by simply locking them in a drawer and forgetting about them.

In the case of your debts, the debt collector is not likely to let you forget. And in the case of your daughter, your conscience, which is your own debt collector, would not let you forget either.

It is an inescapable fact that parenthood comes with a price tag. And whatever the cost, the price must be paid. Often, it must be paid not only in cash and commitment, the commitment of love, time and much labor, but in a real outpouring of blood sweat and tears, not to mention disappointment, and often severe embarrassment. But such is the way of life. Such are the hazards of parent hood."

Sometimes, it became necessary to end on a more conciliatory note, so I would add. "You know there is one commodity that we all possess which we all too often give most sparingly and conditionally when in fact we should be giving it unsparingly, and unconditionally. That commodity is love. The more we give of our love, the more love we would still have to give. For love is a fast flowing stream, the source of which is a volatile, life-giving fountain; singing, and making merry melody along its tireless march toward eternity. For love is sufficient unto love."

I was thinking on these things, and in particular how I could have done well to take a dose of this medicine for myself, in my relations with the troubled girl, when all of a sudden it happened again.

That voice, that same unmistakable voice, so gentle yet so compelling. It hit me so hard that it made me roll off the edge of the bed unto the floor and then sit bolt upright.

"Of course." I said out loud. "I had failed the Musician and I am about to fail this girl now. And as the voice said then and is now saying again, there is something further I could have done; there is something I can do now. Well not actually me; but someone, someone who really cares."

I reached for the bible that I always carried with me. Sometimes when I was alone, particularly in strange far away places, I have always found it a great companion. I opened it now and there, as if directed by Providence, were the words of James, the writer of the Epistle which bears his name.

"Is any among you afflicted? Let him pray. Is any sick among you? Let him call for the elders of the church; and let them pray over him, anointing him with oil in the name of the Lord. And the prayer of faith shall save the sick. The effectual fervent prayer of the righteous man availeth much."

It suddenly occurred to me that during all the time I spent with the Musician I never once mentioned the name of Jesus Christ. Although I was a church-goer, I was never a true witness of the word. Was this the answer to my enigma? The words reverberated in my ears, "Oh, yes there was."

"Thank you Jesus," I said. For I knew there and then, that I had discovered the cure my friend, the girl needed. It was too late for the Musician; but there was time to completely save this girl from the grip of fear that had so overwhelmed her.

The details of how this terrified girl obtained full liberation from the terror and forces of evil and of darkness need not be chronicled here. Suffice it to say that the words of the Gospel of Christ completely freed her from the shackles of fear. For indeed, greater is He that is in us than he that is in the world!

I did not think that the task could have been so easy; but while Jesus was preparing me, the Worker, for the task confronting me when I returned from my vacation, He was also preparing that girl, the Soil, to receive the seeds of the Gospel. According, whenever I look back on the incident, I never for one moment seek to take the credit for helping that girl to overcome her fears, because it was God's Holy Spirit that did it all. For those who have not yet discovered this most important life saving, eternity yielding fact, "Jesus paid it all.!"

Some people say that there is no such thing as a miracle. Recently I heard a Radio Preacher say words to the effect that God does not speak to people in terms of verbalized, audible conversations.

This is not the time or place to traverse such negative averments in specific terms. Suffice it to say, however, that he and the others who think like him, are wrong; very, very, wrong.

God still performs miracles in the lives of believers. And he still speaks to us in clear audible terms.

Sometimes, it is true, we do not hear His voice, because we are too deaf to hear. And all too often, we rationalize away His divine intervention on our behalf, by calling it coincidence or worse still luck. All too often we are content to thank our stars; but not our Maker.

However, it is a fact that as the spiritually blind cannot see the things that are of the spirit, the spiritually deaf cannot hear the things that are of the Spirit.

When God called Samuel by name, he did not hear the voice of God at first, because, he was then spiritually deaf. But in the process of time he became attuned to and compliant with God's commands. Until he became thus attuned he did not hear, but that did not mean that there was nothing to hear.

THE BEGGAR AND THE GIVER

I also knew a woman, who was a beggar. She lived in the country and she could invariably be seen in clean but shabby apparel soliciting alms, from whomsoever, on each and every chance she got. When that beggar woman died she had a deposit account in a bank in the city which at that time and in that locale, many regarded as a small fortune.

I also knew a man from that same village who was known as a Giver. He gave to all who sought his aid or his help. He gave of his money, his time, and his talents, which were not inconsiderable. Among the many objects of his charity was that very beggar woman, who was the frequent recipient of his generosity.

When that man died, there was scarcely enough to pay his funeral expenses.

As I sat one day in the noonday sun, by the side of a little brook, listening to the splashing and gurgling of this fast flowing stream and noting how swiftly smaller fragments move along and are soon carried away and how cumbersome and slow are the larger objects a sudden haze fell over me as a dark cloud blanketed the sun.

In only a few moments later, I was barely conscious of the soft soporific whisper of the breeze as if singing some enchanting lullaby. And thus fanned by its sweet and gently fragrance, as if rocked in the arms of a doting and over indulgent mother, I was quickly transported into the land of dreams.

In my dream, I saw two buses going in opposite directions. On the front of each, in flashing neon letterings, was their respective destinations. On the front of the one were the letters PURGATORY and on the other PARADISE.

On the bus marked Purgatory was the Beggar. She was surrounded by a mean looking mob, all glaring and jeering as she counted her sacks of money. Alas, every one else on the bus knew that the money she had was counterfeit. But she was apparently as oblivious to that fact as she was to her final destination.

That bus which was headed for Purgatory, was in almost total darkness, save for a very dim light shinning directly on the Beggar's face, as if marking her for some special ordeal, in that place beyond called Outer

Darkness, where those that are damned spend eternity. In a few more moments, the bus entered a dark tunnel and I saw it no more.

It occurred to me that the Beggar was probably destined to spend the rest of all eternity, counting, counting, endlessly counting; and it sent cold shivers up and down my spine. "How sad," I sighed. In her case the love of money was to be her passport to a place called Hell.

The other bus, the one marked Paradise, was by way of contrast a kaleidoscope of lights. Its illumination was so pervasive that it gave the illusion that it was not a lighted bus at all, but that the bus itself, was the source of light, as radiant and incandescent as the sun.

All of the occupants of that bus were dressed in white robes as if they were some enchanted choir heading for a stage performance at some large auditorium. Their faces were radiant with happiness, and they laughed and sang to the sound of the sweetest notes of the sweetest music I have ever heard. And lo, the person who was conducting the singing was none other than the Giver from my little village.

As he played his violin of gold, our eyes met briefly; but in that fraction of time, the light and sparkle in his eyes told me that he was in a state of blissful happiness, that only those who have tasted of the waters from the springs of eternal life can know.

At that moment I wanted to get on the bus and join that happy band of pilgrims if only to taste of that living water that had given so much life even to him that had passed beyond the grave.

THE SCHOLAR AND THE ELDER

Part I
The Scholar

I knew a man who, by all accounts, was the offspring of the English Nobility and whose wife was also a noblewoman. He was a goodly man, who, as far as I know, was true to his Godly calling. In any event he rose to the ecclesiastical rank of Canon. He was understandably a scholar, a man of great learning and erudition, which was all too often reflected in his Sunday sermons, although, to be quite frank, not so much in his ordinary, normal, daily discourses.

This, I must say, led to a great deal of speculation, with regard to the source of the materials used in his Sunday sermons. There were those who alleged that he actually purchased them for cash, which I found an odd thing for such a scholarly man to do. There were those who said that much of what he said with much philosophical and intellectual gusto was plagiarized material. But for myself, I, at the time, was more concerned with the substance rather than the form, or the source of what the good Canon had to say.

However, there was one occasion when, in his Sunday sermon, the entire discourse was very reminiscent of and came very close to being a verbatim rehash of a recent political speech by a well known local politician.

This was of course taken by his detractors, as proof positive that his sermons were not his own preparation.

"So what?" I said, in his defense. "If a speech is good enough for a large political out-gathering, it should be good enough for a small religious in-gathering."

The only small criticism I had was that perhaps speech, like newly made wine, would have been more palatable when served, if it were allowed to lie, a little longer, in the barrel at the bottom, of the cellar.

Other than that, I never imputed any impropriety, as it was not my habit of indulging in slurs and innuendos. If a man delivers a sermon, I judged it on its intellectual and spiritual content. I do not go seeking and diving to find out where it came from. My motto being, "omnia praesumuntur rite ese acta." All is presumed to be done decently and in good order.

However, I remember well one particular Sunday, when the quiet, soporific effect of his sermon summoned me to the very edge of slumber. I tried every device and practiced every artifice I could think of, and which had served me well hitherto, in order to convince my members to remain alert.

One particular strategy that had worked well in the past, particularly at those late night parties, was to, using my thumb and forefinger, prop my eye lids open, and keep them in that position until they got so irritated, that the sleep was forced out of them. I tried such a gambit then. But on that occasion, I failed miserably. For while I was thus engaged, the whole system quitted on me.

Now up to this day, I cannot say for sure whether it was the next thing, or the last thing I remembered. But one thing I do know for sure, even though ex post facto. I fell asleep. I woke with a start when, in the midst of my slumber, I heard the resonant voice of the choir master calling out the next hymn.

Embarrassed, I looked around to see if anyone had noticed my temporary lapse. But something in the pew ahead of me caught my eye. It was a note a member sitting immediately in front of me had placed next to her husband. It read simply, "wake me when its over." But unfortunately for both of them, the husband, too had fallen asleep.

Accordingly, I was somewhat gratified to note that, my own lapse notwithstanding, I was singing lustily and the hymn was almost over before the unfortunate couple stirred themselves.

The wife woke first and gave her husband a wickedly sharp nudge in his side with her elbow. He awakened with a start and looked helplessly at his wife. In response, she gave him one of those looks, which clearly said, You wait until we get home."

Well, if looks could kill, that poor man would have died there and then. "Rather you than me, old man," I said to myself, happy to have attended church alone on that occasion.

It is one of the hazards of being the Pastor of a local church. If there is a lack of spirituality, he gets the blame. If members of his congregation take a wink or two during his sermon, he his accused of being dull and uninspiring, which is not necessarily fair to him.

A famous Television Evangelist was fond of telling his audience the following tale. It went something like this.

"Once in one of our long established churches, it happened that while the Preacher was at the height of his sermon, one of the members of the congregation was found to be apparently dead and the paramedics were summoned."

"The paramedics arrived at the church in good time; but it took them a good half an hour searching among the congregation to locate the dead man. That is a good description of a spiritually dead church, he would conclude"

While I do not agree that sleeping, or dying in church for that matter, is conclusive proof of its congregation's spiritual rectitude or lack of it, I wonder, beside us three, how many other somnolent attendants there were in that church on that Sunday.

Thereafter, however, I made it a point never to fall asleep again. I eliminated the Saturday night parties and discos almost entirely, and if I did go out, I made it a point of getting home before midnight. I never fell asleep again; but I did notice that sleeping during the Canon's sermons were so wide spread that it looked a bit more than merely coincidental.

For example, one Sunday, I noticed an old lady sitting in the bench next to me, who appeared to be a very pious and devoted soul. She was fully into the early part of the service, particularly the singing of hymns and canticles, the readings and responses.

However, as soon as the Canon entered the pulpit and said, "In the Name of the Father, the Son and the Holy Ghost, Amen," making the sign of the cross as he repeated the words and imparted the traditional blessing, the old lady withdrew from her hand bag, a little snakes and ladders game set, which she played by herself, until she heard the Canon say, at the end of his sermon, the same words he said at the beginning.

As unhurriedly and as deliberately as before, she then folded the game board, put it away, and prepared herself to participate in the rest of the service. I could not help noticing later, how devoted and matriarchal she looked, as she with arms clasped sedately in front of her, head bowed, and with an air of solemnity, she returned to her seat from the communion table.

Part II
THE ELDER

Some years later, I met another man. He was of humble birth and had no pretensions or claims to nobility. He had no title whatsoever. He was not a preacher, but he apparently loved the Lord and because of his steadfastness and years of good standing in his church he was made an Elder.

As such he would be allowed occasionally to bring the word. I did not know it at first; but later learned that he could neither read nor write. Yet that man delivered one of the finest, most impressive and unforgettable sermons I have ever heard. I am not saying it was the best, or greatest. It certainly was not. But is was undoubtedly, one of the best and more especially, one of the most unforgettable.

He did not once refer to, or read from the bible. He did not back up any thing he said from scripture; his elocution and sermonizing skills left a lot to be desired; but all who heard him would readily recognize that he was inspired and spirit-filled.

Although it s was many years ago, I still remember that sermon as if it were yesterday. This is how he began.

"And the young man said, I would rather suffer affliction with the people of God, than enjoy the pleasure of sin for a season."

He did not refer to the text from which he was preaching; but it was apparent that he was speaking about Moses.

It was equally apparent, too, that the words were taken from Hebrews, chapter 11 where some of the Old Testament Heroes of Faith are chronicled by way of exemplification.

He could not read the bible himself and his choice of words was as limited as his diction was anything but flawless. Yet he was able to touch men's souls. You could not fall asleep in his presence, least of all while he was preaching.

Altogether, it was my privilege to hear him pray on many occasions and preach on about three, he never failed to impress me. I had to sit up and listen each time. If there was a real flaw, as far as I am concerned, it was with regard to his prayers which were somewhat loud and often more than a little repetitive. But long is subjective; and the unburdening of the heart is probably something that cannot be rushed or curtailed. Then, too, perhaps what seemed like long prayers were measured only by my own shortness of spiritual maturity.

What was the difference between the Canon, the man of letters, the man of noble birth, and this simple man who could neither read nor write?

Perhaps the answer lies in the fact that the former spoke from the head, without unction; the latter from the heart under the inspiration of the Holy Spirit. But of course the reader is invited to note carefully the word, perhaps.

THE STRANGER

I also met a man whom I have always referred to as the Stranger for a number of reasons. In the first place, he was a person I had never met before, nor ever since save in my dreams and I never learnt his name or where he was from. But I must say the name "stranger", was given to him more as being descriptive of his behavior, than for any other reason.

I called him strange because that was how his conduct appeared to me at the time. But, in the years to come I was to meet many burdened souls and learn that we all have our individual burdens to bear and that there is no set formula for carrying the weight of oppression and the burdens of life save never to become weary of well doing.

Clearly, the man I call a stranger was one well versed in that very important principle.

He was ascending this very steep mountain road, with a heavy load on his back. Here again, there was nothing peculiar about that fact. I was born and grew up in a rural community in an era when people carried loads on their backs, on their heads, in their hands, and on their mules and asses, whatever was convenient.

What I regarded as being particularly strange about him, was that he was walking backward up this very steep mountain side and he strained, staggered and fell with every step. After each fall, he would struggle to his feet, and start all over, only to fall again.

As I watched his strange behavior, rising, falling, rising and falling again and again, I could not contain myself.

"Sir," I said, more out of curiosity than of pity for the man. "If you need ascend to the top of this mountain with this heavy load, would it not be easier for you to go up frontwards?"

"No," the man replied with the authority and finality of one who knows best and cannot really be bothered to explain to a busybody such as my self.

"But why not?" I persisted. "Surely at least you would be able to see where you are going and so avoid the pitfalls and obstacles which you keep stumbling and falling over."

With a sigh of resignation, the man, still without putting down his burden, and with his back still to the mountain, said, "Son, as you can see, this is a very heavy load. You can also see that this mountain side is very, very, steep."

"Yes," I said eagerly. But waving my interruption aside, he continued.

"I have to reach the top of that mountain. I must. But if I were to turn around and look at the top of the mountain and see how difficult and dangerous is the task ahead and the great distance I would have to travel, well, who is to say? I may get discouraged and give up."

"This way, I just take each step at a time, in faith, knowing that sooner or later, however long it takes and however often I fall, I shall reach the top, if only I do not allow myself to be discouraged."

"I believe that as long as I am not standing still, and I am not retrogressing, I am progressing. It is not the length of the step I take; it is not the rapidity of the progress I make. The thing is to get there."

When I was a boy, I learnt a poem, which has been my constant companion ever since. It taught me that it is perseverance and tenacity, that bring results. For,

"Heaven is not reached at a single bound;
But we build the ladder, by which we rise
From the lowly earth, to the vaulted skies
And we reach to the summit, round by round."
In the words of the man Jesus,
"The race is not for the swift, but he that endures to the end."

"Life for me is a mountain top experience. One can exist in the dull, confining environment of the valley, surrounded by all the restricting influences of the hills and mountains, but never getting even the faintest glimpse of the exhilarating majesty and splendor of land sea and sky when viewed from the vantage point of a great mountain top."

"Only one who has had a mountain top experience could write:-"
"I am Monarch of all I survey,
And my reign no one can dispute.
From the mountain down to the sea,
I am Lord of the fowl and the brute."

"But surely, Sir," I said. "Its all in your mind. You can just not look at the top of the mountain at all. You can just keep going, one step at a time, one day at a time, as you suggest, and pretend its not there and save yourself all the additional anguish, and all those bruises from falling over and over again. Have you not heard that, "So a man thinks, so his?"

That - "Heaven is not reached at a single bound,
But we build the ladder, by which we rise,
From the lowly earth, to the vaulted skies,
And we get to the summit, round by round?"
Again he interrupted me.

"Son," he said. "Each man approaches the difficulties of life in his own way. Your words seem to suggest that your way would be to face life's problems head on. But I not you, am the one carrying this burden. I am the one climbing this mountain. You appear not to approve of my methods. But who are you to approve or disapprove? Who are you to say whether I should face this way or that? Which way is the right way and which way is the wrong way? Is there a right and a wrong way? Who knows what you would do if you were faced with the task of bearing this heavy burden, to the top of such a great mountain?"

"In any event, my way is to take it one step at a time, and if I can, to look the other way, while not giving up. My idea is not how I get there, or how long it takes, or how many bruises I suffer, as long as I get there."

"However, by your own word are you are contradicted. You say correctly, so a man thinks, so he is. Very well, I happen to think that my objective would be better served by approaching this task in a particular way. That is how I think. So by parity of reasoning, that is how I am. I am what I am friend."

"If ever you must needs climb a mountain, whatever the reason for having to do so, you remember this. There is no unique formula, no sine qua non, for the approach to your mountain, save to make sure you get there.

For each man whatever be his creed,
Must his own heavy burden bear.
And oft must sweat and strain and bleed.

So, many and varied are the road that lead to destruction, So, many and diverse are the roads that lead to salvation. But each man is his own keeper. Each man must work out his own salvation, as best he can.

What a strange man, I though, and what peculiar philosophies he espouses? As I walked away he resumed his labored trek up the mountain. And although he fell with almost every step he took, he never gave up.

As I watched him tread his weary way, I though of some lines from a song which I had heard sometime before, and now I was struggling to remember the words, aroused by my encounter with this stranger."

"I saw a way-worn traveler,
In trotted garments clad;
And travelling up the mountain,
It seemed that he was sad.

His back was laden heavy.
His strength was almost gone.
But he shouted as he journeyed.
Deliverance will come."

The encounter with the stranger lingered long in my memory. One night, I dreamt I saw him all bruised and battered and covered with mud and dried blood still trekking backwards, still falling, getting up and carrying on. He had not made a great deal of progress; but he persevered, undaunted.

He started to sing an unfamiliar song, and though I strained to hear the words, I could not do so. Although he was near to me, and singing ever so lustily, his voice sounded ever so far away. So near and yet so far, I told myself. I knew somehow, that the words of the song carried some dreadfully important message. If only I could hear what he was saying! But strained as I did, I still could not hear any words.

The stranger fell again; but this time it was different. For out of nowhere, a man appeared at his side, held the Stranger by the arm, and gently, ever so gently, raise him up. Then he took the Stranger's heavy load on his own back and together, as though the load was a feather, they just floated over dale and hill and in a moment were both sitting on the top of the mountain.

As he took hold of the Stranger and his load, the man looked in my direction with sharp penetrating eyes, the fire within which seemed so bright, that they pierced even to the depth of my very soul, dividing the marrow from the bone, and causing a chill to run the length and breath of my spine.

I will always remember that look. And each time I do, I feel as if I am an ice cube, left on the doorstep of a stranger in the scorching heat of the noonday sun.

It was a look without words; but is was a look that said more eloquently than any number of words could, "Why did you not think of helping the

Stranger, when you had a chance? Surely, your help would have been more constructive than your criticism.

Once in the arms of the other man, the Stranger was no longer singing the strange song. It was as if the song was somehow a song of hope and deliverance and which had its fulfillment in the appearance of that man whose strong arm bore him, first to the top of the mountain and then to the great Divide beyond.

I was to learn the word of that song in later life. It was a very peculiar and almost terrifying twist of faith that lead me to do so; but that is quite another story, the details of which, is better left to be unveiled at a time which is yet to come.

At last, with a look of disdain, the Stranger and his new found friend and deliverer both soared up and up and up until I could see them no more. I never dreamt of the stranger again, although I often though of him with a certain amount of envy, during many a waking moment. There goes, I often said to myself, a vivid reminder of one of those things that come not back, to wit, a neglected opportunity.

On one occasion when I found myself thinking of the Stranger and my strange dream, the following words came to me.

For if the eyes could see the face of fate,
Then would men betimes relent,
And good deeds do, before too late,
They grasp for time, already spent.

As time, once spent, does not return,
As rivers flowed in the briny sea;
So lessons taught and yet unlearned,
Are gone for all eternity.

Know neglected opportunity once it's gone,
Can ne'er be grasped again.
So live each day, and let not one,
Be lost in time or lived in vain.

THE SUICIDE

Some years later, I knew a man who it was thought committed suicide in the face of his financial problems and mountain of debts which had grown out of control. When he died, dozes of unopened letters were found in his desk.

As to be expected, a number of the letters contained bills from his debtors which he refused to open as his particular way of not looking at his mountain. But lots of those unopened letters contained money, money that was owed to him. Money that was sent to him by friends and well wishers who wished to help him out of his problems, but wished to remain anonymous.

It was difficult to thing that he had committed suicide. Ted, for that was his name, was a man who loved life and appeared to live and enjoy it to the fullest. I remember the countless times I would see him at the weekly Bar Be Que bubbling over with laughter, and often champagne, flirting with the ladies and cavorting across the dance hall in his peculiar, if unique bubbly dancing style.

Yet, if the inquest finding was correct, he had set himself and his car on fire, and roasted himself to death in the most cruel and dramatic way. If it is correct to say that "so a man lives, so he dies," then, without questioning the efficacy of that rule, Ted was clearly the exception to it.

No one who knew him, would have associated him with violence of any kind. He was an easy going, fun loving, kind, gentle, and loving man. Without a doubt, he loved life. But perhaps it was that very love that drove him to suicide rather than continuing to live a life devoid of the things that added sparkle and luster and gave meaning and purpose to a life worth living. For him, clearly, life was a glass of Champaign; But Champaign that has lost its bubble, is not fit for the rich, discerning, palate, of the connoisseur.

The report of Ted's death troubled me greatly. He was not a particular friend of mine; but I often met him at many of the galas and fun affairs that took place in and around town. He was a likeable man, and I particularly enjoyed his vitality and his apparent enthusiasm for life and living.

But his death brought back to my mind the encounter with the Stranger and his words. "Each man approaches the difficulties of life in his own way.

Who knows what you would do if you were faced with the task of bearing this heavy burden, to the top of such a great mountain."

Was suicide Ted's way of not facing his particular mountain? It was then that the logic of the Stranger's word began to bear fruit in my own psyche. It is better to take a step, even if you do so with eyes closed and head bowed, than to sit still and do nothing. The real enemy of progress is not slothfulness, but inactivity.

Poor Ted, I thought. I can think of no more horrible way to die or any trespass against the commandments of God more final and more deadly. For even the vilest murderer may be afforded an opportunity to repent and seek forgiveness and secure a place with God in eternity; but the suicide has no hope. For he that dies in his sin remains in his sin for all eternity in permanent alienation from God.

THE OPTIMIST

I used to have a friend whose life philosopher was, "if there is a problem, there is no problem." It was his pat answer to every difficult or knotty situation. It is a statement which appears, at first glance, to be as self defeating as a caption I once saw which said, "if there is a doubt there is no doubt." Neither statements, it is submitted, however, is as contradictory as it may appear to be at first view.

"A problem is only a problem if you worry about it, my friend used to explain. If you can do something about it, then do it. Once done, it is not a problem. If there is nothing you can do about it, ignore it and it will not be a problem for you. Problems are only problems if you make them problems, he used to say."

Of course, I need to explain that, although I have chosen to label this account as the "Optimist", I believe I should call it something, my friend did not regard himself as an optimist. "I am a Realist," he used to say. "When I view a situation, or analyze a circumstance, I look at the substance, not the form."

"Normally, you can expect to find old wine in old bottles, and new wine in new bottles. But often, all too often, these days, men are prepared to put new wine into old bottles and expect us to call it old wine, and old wine in new bottles and attempt to pass it off as new wine."

"The trouble with most people, is, they fail to separate the woods from the trees. They see problems where there is none. Quite often the problems only exist in their minds. More often than not, there is not a problem, in which case people often feel they need to invent one. What exists is a lack of solutions."

"For example," he would say. "A family man has a sick child, in dire need of medicine which he cannot afford to buy. I have a problem," he says. What is the problem? "I have no money."

"In reality, however, what that man has, is not a problem. What he has is the lack of a solution. Why is he unable to buy the medicine? It is not lack of money.

It may be many things but not a lack of money. There is no lack of money in the world. The real difficulty is poor distribution. Some people have too much and some people too little. Those who have too little need to find a way to get their hands on more of the world's money and other resources, just as those who amass wealth spend their whole life inventing and scheming, cheating and stealing, and find ways and means to grab more."

"Maybe he needs a better paying job. Maybe he needs to be more provident and put something aside for a rainy day. Maybe he needs to stop gambling or drinking so much or whatever he otherwise spend his money on. He could also perhaps eat less, spend less on clothes or even move to a cheaper house or apartment"

He would then look me squarely in the face, having bombarded me with a whole series of hypotheses and ask,

"You get the point?"

Of course, I would sometimes, just to be obdurate, argue with him for hours; but there were times when I would concede that all too often we concentrate on trivia to the extent that they do become unnecessarily burdensome.

One almost irrefutable point he was fond of making was this.

"Let us say that there was a difficulty. What would be the best, the most effective, the most efficacious approach to that difficulty? To approach it calmly, rationally and resolutely, not quitting until the best solution is found. Right?" I would concede.

"What if, try as you might, you cannot find any solution. What if there is no apparent way out and the situation is urgent?

"Well," he would say, with a shrug of the shoulder; "you shut it out of your mind and forget about it. Once you have given it your best shot, you close the book. You may open it again and give it another shot at some later date or time. But the clue is, don't worry about it."

"Easier said than done you'd say; so what is the solution? You can lay in bed and toss and turn and fret and pull your hair out and worry from dusk to dawn. But that would not make the problem go away, would it?

On the other hand a good night's sleep has been known to do wonders when, refreshed and energized there from, a rested brain is brought to bear tomorrow, on a difficulty of yesterday."

"Scores of times, I would become bogged down by what looked like the unsolvable clue in a crossword puzzle. But nine times out of ten, the next time I look at that same clue after setting it aside for a while, the answer jumps straight out and grabs me. But the more I agonized over it, the more illusive the answer always seemed to be."

"That is why the ancient of days advise us not to worry. This is what he said.

"Therefore I say unto you, be not anxious for your life, what ye shall eat or what ye shall drink; nor yet for your body, what you shall put on. Is not the life more than food and the body than raiment. Which of you by being anxious can add one cubit unto his stature?"

I must confess that my own philosophy of life is to take the bull by the horn and not let go until either the bull surrenders to my mastery, or it gores me to death. But I do have one immutable rule and it is this. I never allow any bulls within the confines of my bedroom door, day or night.

I once had to judge between two excellent presentations. For the proposition, the words of one poet; "life is but an empty dream." For the opposition, words from another poet; "Tell me not in mournful numbers, life is but an empty dream."

Both presentations were brilliant. I had to make a choice, and with great difficulty I came down in favor of the opposition; but I have always questioned my judgment in doing so. Whether, for example, I had brought to the task at hand the requisite degree of objectivity.

Of course, I was not the sole judge. But of the three, I guess it would be fair to say, I was the most adept at such matters. Accordingly, I was able after much debate to sway the other two, to my point of view, which was not necessarily the correct one.

It might be both instructive and helpful to set out more fully, what the opposing poets wrote says one.
"Life is but an empty dream;
Care destroys the zest of it.
Swift it glideth like a stream.
Mind you, make the best of it."
But says the other.
Tell me not in mournful numbers,
Life is but an empty dream.
For the soul is dead that slumbers,
And things are not what they seem.
Life is real, life is earnest,
And the grave is not its goal,
Dust though art, to dust returneth,
Was not spoken of the soul.
The criteria for judging were well defined and ought not to have been affected one way or another by any personal feelings or other subjective

considerations. And I am not conceding that it was. But even so if the "Resurrectionist" me stole a half point or so from the none "Existentialist" me, I would aver that very little mischief, and hence no grave injustice, was done.

One day, in response to the death of a mendicant, my friend, the Realists said to me. "You know, the state is not concerned with how a man lives, but only with how he dies, unless the man is in a position to pay taxes. And even so, the State is not so much concerned with the man as with getting its hands on his money."

The facts that gave rise to my friend's latest observations were as follows.-

There was living in this little town, a man who was a mendicant, a beggar. He did not work, and his only means of livelihood was to beg. He had no shelter and he would make his nightly abode in the alcove of one of the many government buildings in the town come nightfall.

Ever so often, particularly if he was seen molesting the many tourists who visited the town, he would be arrested and sentenced to prison under the country's vagrancy laws. That way, he would spend at least six months in every year in the local prison, about three months at a time, which was the only shelter and board available to him and the likes of him.

Once when Royalty was do to visit the town, he and all the others, about half a dozen in all, were rounded up and put into prison, so that the streets of the town would be clear of all possible obstacles, and the image of the Country be seen to be untarnished. "After all the Authorities reasoned, the odium of men's conduct can be easily seen; but the stains on men's hands and hearts, and consciences can be easily hidden."

Whatever the motivation, it is a fact that all vagrants were securely locked away. It even happened that a particular woman, not being one of the vagrant class, was on her way to her Sunday worship, when she was offered a ride by the police. Grateful for the lift, she stepped into the police car and was virtually hi-jacked, as she was driven around and round for almost two hours, until the service was well over, in order that she may not disrupt the Royal presence by her untimely and unmelodious singing.

I hardly need to mention that she had committed no crime. Singing too loudly or out of tune, or off key, in church is not an offence. But the police treated her in such a manner, and did so with impunity, because she belonged to that category of humans often described as being "not all there." And there was no one including myself sufficiently brave or conscientious enough to take up her complaint about the grave injustice perpetrated against her by the authorities.

In any event, some time later, the vagrant was found dead, and at that time, the police announced that they suspected foul play and that no stones would be left unturned and no expense would be spared in their effort to determine the cause of death and if murder was the cause, to bring the criminal to justice.

After a great deal of time, effort and money was spent on their investigation, the final verdict was that the vagrant's death was due to natural causes.

"What a waste, my friend commented! A fraction of money would have been better spent on making life a little more tolerable for that poor man, while he yet lived."

"Truly, he repeated his earlier statement. It is not how a man lives; it is now he dies."

My friend's conclusions may not be absolutely supported by his hypothesis; but it does raise the question, why so much fuss is invariably made concerning the death of a man, the sad details of whose life is so often neglected or ignored by all and sundry.

And so it was that a man who had no one to root for him while he yet lived, had a whole country, sparing no expense and losing no small amount of sleep worrying over his death.

A fraction of the money and a little of the concern might have been better spent on the poor man during his lifetime; but the fact that so many was concerned for him and took so great an interest in his death, must have been no small consolation to him, now that he was lying snugly in his grave. He must have been very comforted.

THE ROAD TO CALVARY

Years later, I was reminded of the Stranger when I was saw a film depicting the man Jesus carrying his heavy cross up Calvary Hill. I noted that, unlike the Stranger, Jesus chose to face the Hill, even though His burden was much heavier, as with bowed head and bent back and steps faltering under the weight, he too, staggered and fell.

I noticed too, that, although among the throng who came to see this man, who claimed to be the Son of God, the Savior of the World, there must have been many followers and believers, none apart from one man, made any attempt to help him. And that men was not one of his followers, but a stranger.

I have heard it said that Simon of Cyrene was a black man, and that having opted to be the burden bearer on that occasion, he under took vicariously to make the black man the burden bearer for the rest of mankind all the days of his life. But that is quite another matter.

More to the point, however, I was reminded of the look the man gave me as he was about to help the stranger, and in particular, the scolding and the disdain contained in that look.

But I have learnt one useful lesson. A mountain has many different faces. The only way to get to the top is to start climbing. You may chose to start from any side. It does not matter which. It does not even matter whether you climb up facing frontwards or whether you climb up with your back to the mountain. What is important is to get started and never give up until you reach the summit.

THE MAN JESUS

Finally, I met a man who revealed to me the secret of how to carry a heavy load, any load, up any hill or mountain, without strain and without despair. As I reflect on all of the persons I have met, I realize that life would have been so different for them if they had only met this man also.

I think of the Musician and think how his life could have been spared. I think of the cat-lover and how his love for animals would have been a beautiful thing if only he had love for his fellow man also. I think of my friend and know that there's maybe hope for him yet if he is still alive.

I think of the two priests and hope that if they are both still alive, they have met this man. But, alas if they are dead, they would have met Him before they passed beyond the point of no return. For, there is not reprieve beyond the grave. For I am persuaded that no number of Masses and no amount of prayers for the dead, can in any wise affect, change, or alter the state of those of those who have died. The truth is there is no forgiveness beyond the grave. "For it is appointed to man once to die; and after death the judgment." Reinforcing this point, Jesus said. "For the hour is coming in which all that are in the graves shall hear His voice. And shall come forth. They that have done good, unto the resurrection of life; and that that have done evil unto the resurrection of damnation. (Jn. 5:28-29)

I think of the Stranger and how right he was. Even thought he chose not to face his problem head on, his persistence and faith clearly paid off, when he met the man from Galilee.

I think of the Suicide and how amid all of the fun and frolic of life, he perhaps never heard the word of a loving Jesus who said, "cast you every care on me. That it is faith in God that gives meaning and purpose to human life. That the suicide is a soul lost forever in the darkness and gloom of everlasting torment, in a place called hell.

I think of the Christian, and remember what great ecstasy I felt once the hard, stone-like weight of hate had given place in my heart to a softer, lighter, spirit of love and forgiveness. I wonder if he ever read the passage which says, "no murderer hath eternal life, and pray that he had petitioned God for forgiveness of his sin against me, as I had forgiven him, before he was made to answer the call of the rider of the dark horse.

I think of the Beggar and wonder if she is still counting her counterfeit coins and if she will actually spend all eternity in this way. I wonder too, why no one ever told her, while it was yet day, that, "the love of money is the root of all evil." I often shudder at the thought of her counting, counting, counting, in an endless exercise in futility.

I think of the Giver and wonder if he will remember me when we meet again in those grand celestial mansions. I often wonder whether I would have to improve on my inept guitar strumming, or whether I will have to take lessons when I get there in order to join his choir.

I think of the cat-slayer, and think how lucky it is for him, and for me for that matter, that cats like dogs do not go to heaven. But then, I remember that there are no fast cars there, so that he would not have presented any threat to cats crossing the streets of gold in any event.

I think of the Elder, and wonder if he will get a chance up there to bring the words now and then. I wonder, too, weather he has met Moses, and if the latter had a word or two to say to him.

I think of the tormented girl, and wonder if she is still holding on to that wonderful salvation that she found in so timely a manner.

I think of all the other men and women not mentioned in these passages as well as the untold millions who would be so happy to meet him. His name is Jesus. This is what he said to me, and (sic) to you also.

"Come unto me, all ye that labor and are heavy laden, and I will give you rest. Take my yoke upon you and learn of me; for I am meek and lowly in heart, and ye shall find rest unto your souls. For my yoke is easy and my burden is light." (Mt. 11:28-30).

Each time you see a mountain, standing tall and strong
Let us remember Calvary, where Jesus bore his load.
Whatever be the mountains, We must face in life,
Let us remember the crucified, the perfect sacrifice.
Come unto me ye weary, for I will give you rest,
Come bring your every burden, and lay them on my breast.
When daily cares beset you, there's nowhere else to go,
Let Jesus be your champion, because He loves you so
Just take Him at His promise, for He cannot lie.
Its life or death, the choice, to live or die.

PART IV

A TRIBUTE TO MOTHERS

When long ago in Eden's land
God viewed His proud creation,
He saw at once it could not stand
And so He made a woman.

Alas it was, she first to sin,
And made all men to suffer,
But first she was to know real pain,
For she was the first mother.

A helper she assigned to be,
The man to be her leader,
She plucked his dinner from a tree,
But the fruit was oh, so bitter.

Condemned she was to die, but first,
To know the pain of children.
As Abel's blood cried from the earth.
The mother's heart was broken.

From age to age each mother's breast
Has known the grief and pain,
Of love and labour, life and death,
But rise each day to bear the strain.

And yet her loves' a gem so pure,
It ceases never still to shine.
Through storm and tempest it endure,
A monument so rare, sublime.

What tribute can mere words portray?
What diadem to crown?
A head so worthy to array,
An empress of such great renown.

A woman is a precious gift,
To mankind oft times undeserved.
But a mother is a treasure chest,
She's worth her weight again in gold.

Let every mother be exalted,
Upon a golden, lofty throne.
And let her name be ever honored
For the glory all her own.

Let manhood never dethrone her,
Nor yet despoil her majesty.
The queen of Earth and Ether,
Throughout all eternity.

To all mothers high or lowly,
All mothers rich or poor,
Know that you and you only,
To life's avenues the door.

How precious is a mother's love!
How warm her tender care.
As gentle as a turtle dove,
Are mothers everywhere.

What father can console a child,
Fretfully tossing through the night.
Like a mother strong yet so mild.
From early dusk to the morning light.

And what man there is without a mother.
Though he king or peasant be.
And when there ever was another,
As brave and loving strong as she.

Kings, princes, soldiers, poets,
Philosophers doctors, lawyers
Statesmen, politicians, musicians
Writers, journalists, actors, singers
Psychologists, psychiatrists, lyricists,
Architects, builders, carpenters, masons
Engineers, painters, artist, pages.

Rich man, poor man, scholar, knave
Policeman, doorman, begger, slave
All are your sons! Your sons!
Your sons! Your sons! Your Sons!
Your sons! Your sons! Your Sons!
Your sons! Your sons! Your Sons!
Your sons! Your sons! Your Sons!

Prince John Chaber

PART V

VOICES OF THE HEART

All of these verses came forth out of the bowels of my heart one sad and painful night as I struggled in vain to find answers to, if not make sense of, the sudden and unexpected death of my dearly beloved wife Elsa. It was then, for the first time of my life I truly learned the meaning of deep and painful sorrow.

It was a little more than a year before that I mourned, with Godly sorrow the death of my brother Clyde and I thought then the well-spring of my heart had been truly emptied and that there were no more tears to shed. But now I was learning that the well-spring of the broken heart is both bottomless and fathomless and that tears are gathered there, unknown, but enough to fill a mighty ocean.

It was in the midst of my grief I opened up the doors of my heart and allowed the tears to flow freely and like an effervescent, overflowing fountain it flowed and flowed and in consequence, I was lifted to Calvary as if borne by the waters of a great flood and lodged there at the feet of the Cross which is the crucified Christ. It was there I found comfort and peace and the strength to carry on. It was there that I found meaning in His invitation, "Cast your every burden on me, for I care for you."

It is my most cherished and sincerest wish that some day at some time in some small way, these verses may help someone struggling in like circumstances to find their way out of their sorrow and grief by following the same road I followed led by voices of the heart to find peace with God, on the road to Calvary.

Prince John Chaber

DOWN IN THE VALLEY

I am down in the valley,
Looking up at the stars.
I cannot see the mountain,
I cannot find the stairs.

My heart is full of trouble,
My eyes are wet with tears.
Gloomy, dark shadows surround me,
But still I can see the stars.

Then from beyond the shadows,
I heard a friendly voice.
My son, it said, come follow,
The pathway up the stairs.

And lo, a beam shone round me,
And led me to a hill.
It looked so much like Calvary,
The Cross is right there Still.

Now just a little higher,
And on the mountain I will stand.
And all the days now brighter
For Jesus holds my hand.

Now joyous Hallelujahs,
My soul will shout and sing,
I give all my praises to you,
My Master, Lord and King.

Prince John Chaber

NO FEAR IN DEATH.

I have no fear I'll one day cease to be,
A victim spawned by Adam's truancy.
And though sin reigned by Satan's tyranny,
I know that one day Jesus died for me.
For Jesus loves and cares for me.
He cares for me, He cares for me.
Will be my song eternally

I know that when this earthly frame shall be,
Changed from death to life by God's inerrancy,
When time to time shall be an endless store,
I'll be with Him for all eternity.
For Jesus loves and cares for me.
He cares for me, He cares for me.
Will be my song eternally

Then someday when this troubled life is o'er,
I'll stand victorious on God's celestial shore.
And sing the songs that Angels sing in heaven,
To Almighty God our King, to whom all praise be given.
For Jesus loves and cares for me.
He cares for me, He cares for me.
Will be my song eternally

The lamb shall sit upon His throne,
To welcome all His ransomed people home.
A crown He'll place upon their heads.
Saints called home from life and all the living dead.
For Jesus loves and cares for me.
He cares for me, He cares for me.
Will be my song eternally.

Prince John Chaber

IT IS FINISHED

My heart is singing for my work on earth is done,
And my eyes are looking towards the setting sun.
For soon I'll see that bright and glorious morn,
This darkness tells me soon will appear the dawn.

I scarce can wait to see my Savior's face,
To hear His gentle voice welcome me home
To receive of Him the purest robe of white
To spend eternal presence in His light.

For thou O death is conquered by the grave,
When Jesus, God's Son His precious life He gave.
And death and hell hath no dominion over me,
For Jesus conquered death on Calvary.

Prince John Chaber

The Stairway To Heaven

I am entering the gateway to heaven,
I will walk till the journey's end.
I will climb that golden stairway to heaven
I'll continue to the journeys end.

For the Lord is waiting up there,
At the place He's gone to prepare.
No more pain and despair,
For Jesus is Lord of the air.

I am entering the gateway to heaven,
I will walk till the journey's end.
I will climb that golden stairway to heaven
I'll continue to the journeys end

Prince John Chaber

ON GOOD AND EVIL

Good and evil,
Are not the best of friends,
Though they oft walk hand in hand,
Yet they doth contend
They rely one on the other,
Each to each the control
For better or for worst.

The wheat and the tares,
They grow together
To guile the harvest's hand
Like joy and sorrow,
The doorways to the heart
And though from the other borrow
They never swap their path
Like today and tomorrow.

Love and hate,
Joy and sorrow,
The archetypes of life.
Incorporated from the start,
Like front and back,
Like up and down.
And if ever one be lack,
The other scarce be found.

Prince John Chaber

THEE ONLY LORD

LORD, why do I only think on Thee,
When I am sad and melancholy?
When earthly pleasures are all fled,
And salty tears doth bathe my bed?

LORD, what can I aptly say,
To chase the nightly blues away?
To fix my gaze on things above,
And reliance on a Father's love?

LORD, teach me to live, to walk, to heed.
To know in Thee my greatest need.
That all else beside Thee is but vain
That in Thee I'll find my greatest gain.

Give me the wisdom Lord to see,
In Thee only calm security.
That in the fullness of Thy boundless love,
There's peace and joy forevermore.

Prince John Chaber

TEARS

My tears flowed
Like a broken dam.
My heart pound,
And there's a throbbing in my head.
Because the love of my life is dead,
And sleep has long escaped my bed.

Oh, the woes,
Of a broken heart.
Oh, the pain,
That cruel death imparts.
But wait, what is this I hear?
Tis Jesus whispering, I am near."

This the night,
One month after death,
And still no rest,
Upon my thorny bed.
But the Savior say, "Peace be still!"
"There's rest for the weary and its my will."

My soul is dreary,
I long for rest.
I seek the place,
Land of the blest.
And now I hear the Master say,
"When sorrow's gone, joy will come to stay."

Prince John Chaber

THE DUOS OF LIFE

There is no rainbow,
Until after the rain.
There is no healing,
Until after the pain.

There's no quenching,
Until after the thirst.
There is no second,
Until after the first.

There is no forgiveness,
Until after the sin.
There is no sunset,
Until the day is done.

There is no sunrise,
Until after the night,
There is no darkness,
Until after the light.

There is condemnation,
Until after the crime.
There's no separation,
Until after the union.

There is no returning,
Until after the journey.
There is no rest ,
Until after the labor.

There is no new life,
Until after the resurrection.
There is no salvation,
Before the crucifixion

Prince John Chaber

ODE TO DEATH

O death, thou spoiler of the race,
I assign to thee a place beneath the cross.
Until that day I see thee face to face,
And victory gained and yours the final loss.

O life, that enticeth me to sin,
My Savior's love wantonly to waste.
Thou didst lead me to every dark vale of pain,
But God loves me and in heaven I'll find a place.

O love, the font of grace Divine,
I 'm glad thou wilt not let me go.
For I am His and His forever mine,
I know He's mine and O I love Him so!

O sorrow, cling unto your day,
And flood my dreary heart with care.
But God's dear mercy will chase the pain away,
And joyous day will once again be there.

O Father, I know Thou art in heaven,
And hallowed be Thy matchless name.
And when at last a jeweled crown I'm given,
With Thee forever, will be my final home.

                                        Prince John Chaber

MY REDEEMER

Light of my life, O Thou redeemer blest,
I long to rest my weary soul on Thee.
I'm yearning for the place of my eternal rest,
In the arms of He who loves and cares for m.
O come, Thou come redeemer blest
And let me rest my weary soul on Thee.
Lord of my life, the dearest and the best,
Shine Thy guiding light on me.

Joy of my soul, I am longing for your rest,
This troubled world is naught but pain and grief.
O Thou the hope of all Thy people blest,
No path to Thee save it be found in Christ.
O come, Thou come redeemer blest
And let me rest my weary soul on Thee.
Lord of my life, the dearest and the best,
Shine Thy guiding light on me.

King of my life, the One whom God exalted,
To sit in judgment upon His heavenly throne.
To judge both the living and the dead,
I long for heaven, which is my final home.
O come, Thou come redeemer blest
And let me rest my weary soul on Thee.
Lord of my life, the dearest and the best,
Shine Thy guiding light on me.

Prince John Chaber

NO OTHER WAY

There is no way without Thee,
To chart this storm tossed life.
The winds are full of fury,
The world's awash with strife.
I can but look to Jesus,
The guardian of my soul.
Who is to me most precious,
The one who makes me whole.

There is no life without Thee,
The world is full of sin.
But Christ the King of glory,
Offers hope and peace within.
King Jesus is my fortress,
My joy my resting place.
He is always kind and gracious,
I long to see His face.

Who is the King of glory?
Jesus the Lord Most High,
Oh, hear the wondrous story,
He'll receive us by and by.
One day I'll cross the river,
O'er Jordon I will go,
To be with Him forever,
Because He loves me so.

Prince John Chaber

ANGELS TOLD THE STORY

Angels told the story,
Not so very long ago,
How the King of glory,
Brought peace on earth below.
They told of love and freedom,
Of goodwill toward all men,
Who would enter in His Kingdom,
And let peace on earth begin.

But somehow through the ages,
The message has been lost.
Instead we speak of sages,
Who did not preach the cross.
But when the King of Glory,
One day again appear,
They'll sing the same old story
The angels in the air.

That message on which scorn is cast,
Within the hearts of men,
Who will one day pay the cost,
Too late to hearken then.
But to those His loved and precious,
He will some day give a crown.
The Lord is good and gracious,
He careth for His own.

But He calls men to be faithful,
To the eternal word.
To take to heart the gospel,
That Jesus Christ is Lord.
That when with clouds of glory,
The Lord one day appear,
We'll sing that joyous story,
As we meet him in the air.

Prince John Chaber

SOLACE IN TEARS.

When death removes a dear one,
To a place so far away,
The heart grows dreary and alone,
And cries both night and day.

And though there's love and solace,
In God's eternal word,
We weep until we find a place,
In Jesus Christ, the Lord.

But what if there's separation,
From the Father's love forever?
And there'll never be communion,
With God in heaven ever?

I'm glad that death reminds me,
That I, too, will one day,
Leave the world behind me.
I, too, will pass away.

All hail, the King of Glory!
All hail, the Prince of Peace!
O what a wondrous story,
I'll find in heaven a place.

Prince John Chaber.

A SINNER'S PRAYER

Lord, I'm vile and stained with sin,
I cannot turn to Thee,
Unless your mercy draws me in,
And Jesus smiles on me.

Lord teach me to pray aright each day,
Hold me in Godly fear.
So I will never lose my way,
Because your love is near.

Lead me to the cross where Jesus died,
Reveal His perfect life to me.
Show me His hands, His Feet, His side
Take my through Calvary.

That in His life, I'll see the light,
That is his Wounds the sacrifice,
That in the empty tomb the linen cloth,
The angel's words, He is in Paradise.

Jesus, till your smiling face I see,
Keep me constant, fixed on thee,
Till in the fullness of your love,
I lose myself in things above.

Prince John Chaber

JESUS IS CALLING

Heavenly showers around me falling,
May I fix my gaze on Thee.
I hear a voice and it is calling,
Oh, thou sinner come to me?

Heavenly sunbeams warm my life,
On a cold and wintry day.
My heart is burdened down with grief
I cannot keep the tears away.
Still I hear the voice of Jesus calling,
Oh, thou sinner loves thou me?

The dew of heaven makes me shiver,
In the dark and dreary night.
And my thoughts turn to the giver,
Of the darkness and the light.
Still I hear the voice of Jesus calling,
Oh, thou sinner loves thou me?

A voice from heaven calls my name,
Tis the Savior's gentle voice I hear.
I am naked but not ashamed,
Because Jesus loves me dear.
I hear His voice of comfort calling
Leave the world and follow me.

Prince John Chaber

THE KEEPER OF MY SOUL

What if the keeper of my soul,
Is the one who cares and dies for me?
What if Jesus makes me whole,
By His death on Calvary?

And what if constant by His side,
Is the Lord of heaven and earth?
And what if all my needs provide,
The one who truly gave me birth?

And what if all my doubts and fears,
By God's love are all cast away?
What if all my sorrows and cares,
By God's grace have lost their sway?

And what if pestilence and pain
Are all covered by His blood?
And what if the enemy strives in vain?
By tribulation, fire and flood?

And what if now no condemnation,
What if my place in Him is sealed?
And what if now no separation?
Can remove my strength and shield?

And what if every day victorious,
No more a slave to death and sin?
I hear His voice so sweet and glorious.
Bid me gently, "Enter in?"

Prince John Chaber

LITANY

How can I know my Savior died?
How can I see His wounded side?
How can His hands, His feet I see?
By prayer and fast and Litany.

How can I see the empty grave?
How can I share the life He gave?
How can I see the linen cloth?
By prayer and fast and Litany.

Lord Jesus Thou didst die for me.
You gave your life on Calvary
So may I always look to Thee,
By prayer and fast and Litany.

Jesus o'er death triumphantly,
You loosed the chains of tyranny.
And by the cross lifted me,
From death to life eternally.

Prince John Chaber

PART VI

The two poems following were first published in a book by this author entitled, Understanding Forgiveness. It would seem appropriate to include them here so that this may provide a more complete compendium of his work as a poet. It is the author's hope that these two poems will have the desired effect.

IN MEMORIAM

The face of terror raised its head,
Our sons and daughters now are dead!
And who will weep for them?
We will weep for them!

Demonic men broke through our door,
And mamas and papas are no more.
And who will sing lullaby's for them?
We will sing for them!

Fiends! They came in demented rage,
Sent grandmas and grandpas to the grave!
And who will pray for them?
We will pray for them!

What deathly force those cowards ushered!
Taking with them our sisters and brothers!
And who will speak for them?
We will speak for them!

Without warning came they like wolves!
Wreaking havoc on our friends!
And who will judge for them?
We will judge for them!

As for the dead, what pain they felt?
As twisted steel, bricks, mortar melt!
And who will bury them?
We will bury them.

They came! They demolished our beautiful city!
Bespoiled our buildings without pity!
Defenseless all they lived, they died.
They got no pity when they cried!
And who shall avenge them?
We will avenge them!

And that date, eleventh September,
We will always, always, remember!
And who will repay the cowards?
We will repay them, a thousand fold.

And we, the living,
We will weep for them.
We will sing for them.
We will pray for them.
We will speak for them.
We will judge for them.
We will bury them.
We will rebuild for them.
We will avenge them.
We will remember them,
And infinitum, in memoriam!

Prince John Chaber

WE STAND

We stand beneath the stars and stripes,
One nation under God.
We brace our shoulders for the fight,
And we will not be moved.
We will not be moved.
We will not shrink from duty's call
No matter what the cost!
We will rise each time we fall.
We will not suffer loss.
Onward forward,
Marching with the flag we go,
Onward forward,
Proudly 'neath the flag we go!

   2. Our cause is just; we need not fear,
God is on our side.
Our nation's pledge to Him is clear.
We'll stem the surging tide.
Our freedom we'll not sacrifice
Our justice we'll defend!
Our honor stands at any price.
We'll hold out to the end!
Chorus Onward forward,
Marching with the flag we go!
Onward, forward,
Proudly 'neath the flag we go!

   3. The enemy is but Satan's kin,
No matter what they say.
We will fight them, we will win,
We'll resist them all the way.
There is no prize that has no pain,
No cross without a crown.
No labor lost if there be gain.
And the battle's not our own!

Chorus Onward forward,
Marching with the flag we go,
Onward, forward,
Proudly 'neath the flag we go!

4. Onward Christian pilgrims stand,
Unite against the foe,
We must drive them from this land
And let the whole world know.
The God of our fathers, is the One,
The wind beneath our sail!
When evil stalks our peaceful home
We'll fight and we'll prevail.

Chorus Onward forward,
Marching with the flag we go,
Onward, forward,
Proudly 'neath the flag we go!

5. This our land our Father's land,
Home of the brave and free
This our land our children's land
And ours their liberty
We will break the enemy's line
By land, or air, or sea,
Hurrah, hurrah, hurrah, hurrah,
We'll shout for victory.

Onward forward,
Marching with the flag we go,
Onward, forward,
Proudly 'neath the flag we go!

Prince John Chaber

ODE TO HAITI

Toussaint, thou indomitable warrior,
Fearless leader of your race,
Your country struggles with bitter sorrow.
Send forth, your strong eternal spirit,
And let their broken spirits soar,
And find hope in your strength and merit.
Let the cry of the widows and orphans,
The sick, the wounded and the homeless,
Find solace in your precious memories.
Cry out to God, thou great and loyal son,
Let not the foundation you so deftly built,
Be made void by tragic fate or cataclysmic ruin.
Arise my Haitian brothers, join hand in hand,
And step by step, brick by brick, build a brand new land

Prince John Chaber